USING
BOOKS
AND
LIBRARIES

PRENTICE-HALL INTERNATIONAL, INC., *London*
PRENTICE-HALL OF AUSTRALIA, PTY. LTD., *Sydney*
PRENTICE-HALL OF CANADA, LTD., *Toronto*
PRENTICE-HALL OF INDIA (PRIVATE) LTD., *New Delhi*
PRENTICE-HALL OF JAPAN, INC., *Tokyo*

USING BOOKS AND LIBRARIES

Fifth Edition

ELLA V. ALDRICH

Prentice-Hall, Inc., Englewood Cliffs, New Jersey

FOREWORD

This manual was originally written for the freshman course in library use at Louisiana State University. Upper classmen and graduate students have also found it useful, especially where no provision exists for advanced instruction in bibliography. An effort was made, first of all, to prepare it within the vocabulary range of the average freshman, and then to make it readable and informative.

In the present edition, the book has been completely revised and enlarged. It should be usable by any college or university student, whether or not he has had previous library experience.

The course is successfully related to actual library use by a term bibliography, for which work sheets in the back of the textbook are to be prepared. Each student selects a subject of interest to him; and while he studies each group of reference books, the card catalog, and the periodical and other indexes, he searches for relevant material. As he locates it, he records his references on the work sheet corresponding to the lesson. The number of references from the card catalog and from the indexes will depend upon the organization of the course and upon the judgment of the instructor. An assignment of five references from the card catalog and one from each periodical index has proven satisfactory in several schools. A person prominent in the field of the student's bibliography subject may be chosen for the biographical reference.

Completed pages are torn out during the semester, revised by the instructor, and returned to the student for his compilation of the term bibliography. This practice gives meaning to the course and does away with isolated "problems," too frequently adopted from library schools for college instruction. However, special problems may be prepared for History, Literature, and Religion because recently developed subjects rarely appear in references covering those fields.

This manual affords a *basis* for instruction and study. Supplemented by the imagination and interest of the instructor, it will help to develop a course rich in the possibilities of such instruction. Its flexible design will enable the instructor readily to meet the needs of his institution.

In preparing this revision, the author was advised and aided by a number of specialists, to whom she wishes to express gratitude. Mrs. Jackie Ducote, her research assistant, deserves a special accolade for a fine accomplishment. Indispensable assistance was received from members of the library staff and from the faculty of Louisiana State University: Miss Alice Hebert, Head, Department of Books and Libraries, and her two assistants, Mrs. Katherine K. Thomas and Miss Rosalie V. Lindsey; Mr. Theodore N. McMullan, Director of the Library; Miss Elizabeth Tarver, Chief Cataloger, and her assistant, Mrs. Millicent M. Hennigan; Mrs. Helen H. Palmer, Mrs. Anne Jane Dyson, and Mrs. Mary-Jane F. Kahao of the Humanities Division; Mrs. Marguerite M. Hanchey of the Sciences Division; Mrs. Edith F. Hill and Mrs. Katherine P. Hood of the Social Sciences Division; Mrs. Jennie Beth S. Clark, Librarian of the Library School; Mr. Joseph H. Mattox, Jr., Director of Public Relations, and his assistant, Mr. Oscar Richard, who are responsible for the cover design.

Ella V. Aldrich

CONTENTS

USING
BOOKS
AND
LIBRARIES

COLLEGE AND UNIVERSITY LIBRARIES

An old story of library regulations at Brown University tells us that students came to the library four at a time when sent for by the librarian and were not allowed to go beyond the librarian's table on penalty of threepence for each offense!

The college or university library of today is not the sheltered, awe-inspiring place it was even twenty-five years ago. It is the hub of a wheel whose spokes reach into every department of the institution. No college or university can develop or produce effective work without a strong library as its center. An educational institution is rated largely by its library.

Educational methods have changed and broadened so that both faculty and students are dependent upon the library. A knowledge of the use of the library is essential, not only to get the most out of the whole college experience, but to save time.

No person of normal intelligence would attempt to pilot a plane or swim in deep water without knowing how. The best way to learn any skill is through instruction and practice. Thus, in library use you learn *how to find information quickly and easily* through instruction and practice. The average freshman has had limited library experience. Naturally, his first trip to the college library is bewildering. The students there seem so busy. He wonders if they know how to find what they are looking for; and if so, how long it took them to learn.

1

Rules and Regulations

The routines and regulations of most college and university libraries are similar, but each has its own variations. They are usually mimeographed for distribution at the Circulation Department, and are printed in the student handbooks of some institutions. They may also appear in a special library handbook.

Divisional Arrangement

For some twenty years librarians have been studying library arrangement in terms of services to instructional and research needs. Many postwar college and university libraries have been planned to meet such needs, providing a more adequate approach to subject fields by arranging the collection of library materials in *divisional* reading rooms with all books, periodicals, pamphlets, reference books, and reserve books covering a certain area of knowledge in a *division* of the library. All of these materials are on open shelves or stacks from which the library's user may select his choices instead of presenting a call slip at a circulation desk for someone to get the materials for him. In such an arrangement there are usually circulation desks or check points at exit doors of the library.

Typical *divisions* are Humanities, Social Sciences, and Sciences. In addition, there are usually other departments such as Government Publications, Newspapers (with microfilm readers in an adjacent room), Archives and Rare Books, and a Record Collection with near-by soundproof listening rooms.

Each division has its own staff of library specialists to serve the public with reference work and to assist in locating books, periodicals, reserve books, and pamphlets. In some libraries each division has its own card catalog in addition to the general or central catalog on the entrance floor. Others have only the central catalog, which lists the entire holdings of the library.

Knowledge of the *location* of library materials *by division* is obtained from the classification number of each item—in other words, certain classifications of books and other materials are shelved in the division to which they relate.

However, some libraries with the divisional arrangement have found that it is necessary, more convenient, and less subject to loss to have a Reserve Book Department instead of housing reserve books in pertinent divisions.

Traditional Arrangement

CIRCULATION OR LOAN DEPARTMENT

Some kind of qualifying evidence is usually necessary for the privilege of borrowing books. It may be a borrower's card, a bursar's receipt, or a registration card. Where the library has an electric "charging" machine, you must present a borrower's card each time you borrow or renew books or other material, because your card has a metallic plate with *your* number, which is automatically stamped on the cards from a book to show that you have it. Other libraries require different means of identification, and a "call slip" must be filled out with the call number of the book (see page 32), the author and title, and, finally, your name and address. These slips are available at the card catalog or at tables near the card catalog.

Except for reserve books (see below), most books are loaned for a period of two weeks and may be renewed for a similar period. Periodicals, government publications, and theses and dissertations are usually loaned for Reading Room use only. A card or a date slip in the back of the book shows when a book is due. Keeping up with that date will save you money! The fine for overdue books varies from five cents a day in some colleges and universities to twenty-five cents in others. If you have difficulty with borrowing procedure, ask for help at the Circulation Desk or at some other department designated for such assistance—the Information Desk, the Reference Department, or the Readers' Adviser. Some libraries have "Catalog Advisers" who explain the intricacies of the card catalog and of borrowing procedure.

RESERVE BOOK DEPARTMENT

The professor says, "Read chapters two and three in Hazen's *Modern History of Europe,* on reserve in the library." What does "on reserve" mean? Just this: much of your college work will be done through assigned readings in books other than your texts. Some libraries reserve these books for your use in a special department; others circulate them from the Loan Desk. The commonly practiced policy is that they may not be taken from the library during the day and only with permission for overnight, a weekend, or holidays. The fine for overdue reserve books is usually more than for two-week books, for obvious reasons. A great many people must use a comparatively small number of books, which should therefore be available at all hours. Further, a time limit is often placed upon the use of reserve books during the day. Around examination time it works a hardship on students who have neglected supplementary reading, but it is altogether a good regulation.

In a few universities, a rental reserve collection, very limited in size, serves as an emergency alternative for those who find it impossible to observe reserve book regulations.

REFERENCE DEPARTMENT

Where *would* I look for information about Bee Culture? Is there any chance of my finding records of Olympic Games? If you have no idea where to look for information, or if you cannot find it after some searching, ask the Reference Librarian, who will be glad to help you.

If the library has a special Reference Room, around its walls are shelved reference books—encyclopedias, handbooks, dictionaries, and other books covering general fields and specific subjects. Libraries without a Reference Room utilize a portion of one of the reading rooms for the Reference Department. The same arrangement is often made for the Reserve Book Department.

PERIODICAL DEPARTMENT

How do you keep up with what's going on? Through magazines and newspapers, of course. The current or most recent issue of each magazine subscribed to by the library is shelved in alphabetical order, usually, in the Periodical Room. The latest issues of newspapers are also here. These two types of material rarely circulate for home use, even when bound in complete volumes like books, because it is often impossible to replace them and research suffers from broken sets.

In some libraries, bound volumes of the most frequently used periodicals may be shelved in the Periodical Room. Other libraries have only current issues there. In the latter case, you must call for earlier numbers at the Periodical Desk or the Circulation Desk, depending upon the policy of the library.

BROWSING ROOM

All work and no play isn't good for anyone. Reading for fun is something you can't afford to miss in college, especially when all you have to do is to select a book from the shelves in the Browsing Room. If you don't find exactly what you want, the Readers' Adviser will help you, even to the point of ordering books on subjects not found in the collection. Use this room as you would your own library.

The regulations of the individual library will reveal whether or not the books circulate for home use. At Dartmouth, Yale, Harvard, and California, the "Browsing Room" is lavishly comfortable, with many expensively and handsomely bound books. In some libraries the room for recreational reading is very informal and simple; its collection circulates for home use. Today most libraries make some provision for this type of reading. Where there is no Browsing Room, the need is met by a Browsing Corner or a few shelves of books near the Circulation Department.

DEPARTMENTAL LIBRARIES

The departmental libraries in some universities and colleges, serving as branches of the main library and limited to special fields, are located in the respective departments. All books in the departmental libraries are represented in the card catalog in the main library. Unless the general library has duplicate copies, you must go to a departmental library to borrow its books.

Our best college and university librarians are not in agreement as to whether it is better to keep all books under one roof in specialized departments or to spread departmental libraries over the campus, thereby decentralizing the book collection and having it near the departments they serve. The most recent system is the former, with divisional reading rooms.

INTERLIBRARY LOAN

An important service rendered by libraries is called "interlibrary loan." Libraries lend each other rare source-materials needed by students and faculty for research or study. This service is not limited to books and other printed matter; microfilms, theses, and the like may also be loaned. Naturally, the carrying charges must be paid by the borrower.

However, interlibrary loan by mail is a slow and clumsy process. New, mechanized forms of communications systems among libraries are now entering the library picture. (See below)

MICROFILM DEPARTMENT

With the progress of microphotography, small films of books, periodicals, and newspapers, or of certain sections of them, may be borrowed by students and faculty to be read with a machine that magnifies them to normal size. Manuscripts, rare books, and many other types of printed or written materials can be microfilmed for researchers.

Many libraries are developing large collections of such films, especially of *The New York Times* and other newspapers. Microfilms are a great space-saving device.

AUTOMATION

For some years libraries have had materials microfilmed, have had electric "charging" machines; but now most libraries of appreciable size also have Xerox and other copying machines available for faculty, students, and researchers.

Another facet of automation has been developed whereby a group of libraries (and it can eventually become national) can cooperate in a new communications system called Long Distance Xerography (LDX). With this development member libraries can get Xerox copies of needed materials from each other within a matter of minutes by telephone and the proper machines.

It is obvious what tremendous financial savings can be effected! Participating libraries can decide on fields of specialization for expensive, rare, or scarce research materials and prevent costly duplication by other libraries. LDX can make such items available to any or all of the libraries within minutes.

Computers are increasingly important to libraries in many of their functions—clerical functions, producing book catalogs, maintaining serial records, accelerating the acquisitions process, etc.

Automation has come to libraries and will bring many changes to their structures and functions.

THE
BOOK

A broken back shortens the life even of a book. Have you seen a person open a book, especially a new one, and bend it back so sharply that it cracked? Each book received by a library is opened carefully. It is held with the backbone flat, and each cover is opened and a few pages pressed down, first from the front and then from the back, until the whole book is gone through. Open books should not be put face down; neither should the place be marked with a thick object.

Parts of a Book

Understanding the parts of a book saves time. Skill in the intelligent use of books can be developed easily, and is much more satisfactory than the "hunt and peck" system.

TITLE PAGE

The first important printed page in a book is the title page. Besides the full name or title of the book, it gives the author, place or places of publication, publisher's name, and usually the date of printing.

Title. The full name of a book always appears on the title page. Occasionally it is fuller or longer than the title on the back of the book because it includes a descriptive phrase or *subtitle*—as, *A Christmas Carol in Prose; Being a Ghost Story of Christmas.* In listing titles in a bibliography, be sure to use the one on the title page.

Author. The list of degrees after an author's name, especially in nonfiction books, is a clue to his standing as an authority. Occasionally a few of his most important works may be given.

Editors, Compilers, Illustrators, Translators. If anyone of importance besides the author is responsible for the book, his name also appears on the title page—for example, an outstanding critic *editing* an author's works, an illustrator of note, or someone collecting or compiling the stories, poems, or essays of a number of authors.

Editions and Reprints. All copies of a book printed from a set of plates make up an *edition.* If more copies are printed later from the same plates, the book has been *reprinted.* But if any changes are made in the book, either bringing it up to date or adding material, it is called a *new* or *revised edition.* In science and many other subjects, it is important to have the latest edition.

Publisher. If a publisher specializes in a certain kind of book, his name on the title page suggests the excellence of the work. The same applies to almost any book printed by a publisher of established reputation.

COPYRIGHT

Copyrighting a book is like patenting an invention. It guarantees ownership and protection in publishing for a period of twenty-eight years, with the privilege of renewal for a similar period. The copyright date verifies the first publication of the book in the United States; it usually appears on the back of the title page. For famous books that have been printed in many editions, the copyright date indicates only the first appearance of that particular edition. An author copyrighting a book must deposit two copies in the Library of Congress in Washington and pay a fee for copyrighting.

PREFACE OR FOREWORD

In the preface or foreword the author states his purpose in

writing the book and expresses indebtedness to those who assisted him.

CONTENTS

The table of contents near the front of the book cannot be used as or take the place of an index. It is merely a list of the chapters or parts of the book, occasionally including a summary or analysis of each chapter.

ILLUSTRATIONS, MAPS, ETC.

A list of pictures, maps, and other illustrations, in the order of their appearance in the book, helps the reader locate one of them quickly.

INTRODUCTION

The introduction differs from the preface in that it is about the *subject matter* of the book. It prepares the reader for the content of the book or interprets it to him. It is important in understanding the book and should not be passed over.

TEXT AND NOTES

The main part of the book is the text. Explanatory material in the form of notes frequently appears at the bottom of the page (footnotes), at the end of the chapter, or at the end of the book. The same small printer's mark is used in the text and beside the note to which it refers.

GLOSSARY

A glossary is a list of uncommon words, technical terms, or words with a special meaning for a science, an art, a dialect, or some other work. It should not be confused with a *vocabulary* in a foreign grammar.

APPENDIX

Many instructors expect you to know material found not only in footnotes, but also in an appendix. The latter is supplementary or added material that cannot be introduced easily into the text, such as tables, notes, and bibliographies.

BIBLIOGRAPHIES

A bibliography is a list of references—books, magazine or news-paper articles, manuscripts, documents, pamphlets, and so forth—often appearing at the end of a chapter, at the end of a book, or at the end of an article in an encyclopedia or other reference book. Frequently the material printed on an important subject is so extensive that the list fills a whole book. People who plan to specialize in a subject should find out what *bibliographies* have been printed in that field. Many such reference lists have descriptive notes which help in selecting the best books or other materials. These are called *annotated* bibliographies. A *subject bibliography* is a list of references on a certain subject; an *author bibliography* is a list of an author's works.

INDEXES

Do you "thumb" through a book to find what you want? That is like sharpening your pencil with a knife when a mechanical sharpener is at hand. In comparison, an index saves even more time. It is an alphabetical list of everything of importance treated in the book, and is usually found at the end of the book. An index saves time by locating information buried somewhere in the book and by preventing fruitless searching for information *not* treated in the book.

TYPES OF INDEXES

The most common type of index is the *general* index of names, subjects, titles, and so forth. In some books, it is broken up into several indexes: for example, a *subject* index, a *title* index, and an *author index.* Collections of poetry usually include a "*first line*" index. Be sure to notice the type of index if the book has more than one. Each volume in a set of books may have an index, but a general index usually appears in the last volume. In a general index the volume number is indicated in Roman numerals to distinguish it from the page number. Some sets of books group their information under large subjects, and a general index is the only clue to their subdivisions or small subjects. Frequently the set is published over a period of years, and up-to-date material is included in the later volumes with no plan for it at the beginning, in the earlier volumes. This new material is, therefore, not referred to by cross references. You can see the necessity of consulting the index volume to get every bit of needed information. The following list of a few of the references under Industrial Hazards is from the index volume of the *Encyclopaedia of the Social Sciences:*

INDUSTRIAL HAZARDS—vii 697–705; Accidents, Industrial i 391–401; Automobile Industry ii 327 a; Cement iii 290 a; Child (Labor) iii 422 a; Clerical Occupations iii 552 b;

Only two of the above references are listed among the cross references at the end of the article "Industrial Hazards," which shows the importance of consulting the index volume.

A *cumulative index* is one that becomes larger by successive additions. This is true of indexes to periodicals, which are published each month and then *cumulate* into an annual volume by adding together all of the monthly indexes into a single index, all in one alphabet. The same is true of some yearbooks which cumulate the index every few years to reveal information found in previous volumes.

CROSS REFERENCES

Very often two or more words mean exactly or nearly the same thing. The page references (in an index) cannot be entered under every one of these synonymous subjects; therefore, it is necessary to provide some device to assist people who would each look under a different word. This device is called a *cross reference,* because it leads across to the subject in the index where the desired information is listed: for example, *Farming, see Agriculture.*

Another type of cross reference is the *see also* reference, which tells where *additional* material can be found; for instance, *Farm Buildings, see also Agricultural Engineering; Barns; Stables.* Be sure to follow up a cross reference in order to get all of the information you need. Besides being useful in indexes, they are an indispensable device in alphabetically arranged books and card catalogs.

CLASSIFICATION AND ARRANGEMENT OF BOOKS

CLASSIFICATION

Since it is convenient and important to keep together all books on a subject, libraries have a device that makes such grouping possible. It is a classification system that groups books according to *subject,* thereby bringing together on the shelves all books on a given subject, such as Agriculture, or Radio, or Aviation. There are many systems for classifying books, but the two most generally found in libraries are the Library of Congress Classification and the Dewey Decimal Classification. The former uses the letters of the alphabet to classify books; for instance, S is for agriculture. The most common system, however, is the Dewey Decimal, which assigns a number to each book. For example, 631.2 stands for *Farm Structures* and all books on that subject will have that number and stand together on the library shelves.

Dewey Decimal Classification

Dewey divides all knowledge into nine major classes, with an extra class for works so general as to make a definite place in any of the nine classes impossible:

000 GENERALITIES
   010 Bibliographies and catalogs
   020 Library science
   030 General encyclopedic works
   040
   050 General periodicals
   060 General organizations
   070 Newspapers and journalism
   080 General collections
   090 Manuscripts and book rarities

100 PHILOSOPHY AND RELATED DISCIPLINES
   110 Ontology and methodology
   120 Knowledge. cause, purpose, man
   130 Pseudopsychology, parapsychology, occultism
   140 Specific philosophic viewpoints
   150 Psychology
   160 Logic
   170 Ethics (Moral philosophy)
   180 Ancient, medieval, Oriental philosophy
   190 Modern Western philosophy

200 RELIGION
   210 Natural religion
   220 Bible
   230 Christian doctrinal theology
   240 Christian moral and devotional theology
   250 Christian pastoral theology, parishes, religious orders
   260 Christian social and ecclesiastical theology
   270 History and geography of Christian church
   280 Christian denominations and sects
   290 Other religions and comparative religion

300 THE SOCIAL SCIENCES
   310 Statistical method and statistics
   320 Political science
   330 Economics
   340 Law
   350 Public administration
   360 Welfare and association
   370 Education
   380 Commerce
   390 Customs and folklore

400 LANGUAGE
   410 Linguistics and nonverbal language
   420 English and Anglo-Saxon
   430 Germanic languages
   440 French, Provençal, Catalan
   450 Italian, Romanian, etc.
   460 Spanish and Portuguese
   470 Italic languages
   480 Classical languages and modern Greek
   490 Other languages

500 PURE SCIENCES
   510 Mathematics
   520 Astronomy and allied sciences
   530 Physics
   540 Chemistry and allied sciences
   550 Earth sciences
   560 Paleontology
   570 Anthropological and biological sciences
   580 Botanical sciences
   590 Zoological sciences

600 TECHNOLOGY (APPLIED SCIENCES)
   610 Medical sciences
   620 Engineering and allied operations

630 Agriculture and agricultural industries
640 Domestic arts and sciences (Home economics)
650 Business and related enterprises
660 Chemical technology, etc.
670 Manufactures processible
680 Assembled and final products
690 Buildings

700 THE ARTS

710 Civic and landscape art
720 Architecture
730 Sculpture and the plastic arts
740 Drawing and decorative arts
750 Painting and paintings
760 Graphic arts
770 Photography and photographs
780 Music
790 Recreation (Recreational arts)

800 LITERATURE AND RHETORIC

810 American literature in English
820 English and Anglo-Saxon literature

830 Germanic languages literature
840 French, Provençal, Catalan literatures
850 Italian, Romanian etc. literatures
860 Spanish and Portuguese literatures
870 Italic languages literature
880 Classical and modern Greek literatures
890 Literatures of other languages

900 GENERAL GEOGRAPHY AND HISTORY, ETC.

910 General geography
920 General biography, genealogy, etc.
930 General history of ancient world
940 General history of modern Europe
950 General history of modern Asia
960 General history of modern Africa
970 General history of North America
980 General history of South America
990 General history of rest of world

Each major class is divided into ten smaller classes, each of which includes ten still smaller classes for further subdivisions of the main subject. Decimal expansion then makes it possible to provide a place for the smallest topic, as shown under 635.9 below:

600 TECHNOLOGY (APPLIED SCIENCES)

610 Medical sciences
620 Engineering and allied operations
630 Agriculture and agricultural industries
  635   Garden crops (Horticulture)
  635.9 Flowers and ornamental plants (Floriculture)

635.91   Production
635.92   Injuries, diseases, pests, and their control
635.93   General and taxonomic groups
635.931 Annuals and biennials
640 Domestic arts and sciences (Home economics)
650 Business and related types of enterprise
660 Chemical technology
670 Manufactures processible
680 Assembled and final products
690 Buildings

CALL NUMBERS

Having a number of books on the same subject, and therefore with the same class number, makes it necessary to distinguish among them in some way. This is done by combining
a "book number" with the class number to make up the "call
number" of the book—the number by which you call for a book
at the Loan Desk and by which it is located on the shelf. The
book number is composed of the first letter or two in the
author's last name plus a number from the Cutter table of
author numbers. Very often the first letter in the title of the
book is then added. For instance, H. Harold Hume's number
is H88. Hume wrote *Azaleas and Camellias,* the class number
for which is 635.9; and the combination of the *class number*
and the *book number* is the *call number* of the book,

$\frac{635.9}{\text{H88a}}$. The letter *a* in the book number distinguishes this book

from the author's *Gardening in the Lower South,* whose call

number is $\frac{635.9}{\text{H88g}}$.

This system makes it impossible for two books to have the
same combination of numbers. The call number appears on
the book and in the upper left corner of every card for that
book in the card catalog.

ARRANGEMENT

The arrangement of books on the shelves reads from left to
right on each shelf and from top to bottom of the stack (sec-

tion or group of shelves). The call numbers are read numerically, and decimals are valued just as in mathematics.

Library of Congress Classification

The Library of Congress Classification is used by many libraries with large collections, and it is becoming increasingly popular with university, state, and federal libraries, especially since they want to apply to their own libraries any uses of automation made by the Library of Congress. However, if a university library collection has grown to considerable size using the Dewey Decimal Classification, it would be prohibitively expensive to change to the Library of Congress Classification.

This classification system utilizes the letters of the alphabet combined with arabic numerals to classify library materials. A brief summary of this system follows:

A	General Works. Polygraphy	N	Fine Arts
B	Philosophy. Religion	P	Language and Literature
C	History—Auxiliary sciences	PN	Literary History and
D	History and Topography		Literature (General)
	(except America)	Q	Science
E-F	America	R	Medicine
G	Geography. Anthropology.	S	Agriculture, Plant and
	Folklore. Sports.		Animal Industry
H	Social Sciences	T	Technology
J	Political Science	U	Military Science
K	Law	V	Naval Science
L	Education	Z	Bibliography and Library
M	Music		Science

The twenty-one main classes are represented by capital letters used singly. Main divisions are represented by two capital letters, as illustrated under class P in the outline above. Topics under the classes and divisions are developed by the use of arabic numerals in ordinary sequence from 1 to 9999, according to the need for detail. An illustration below from class S, Agriculture, shows how it is possible to provide a place for the smallest topic:

S   AGRICULTURE (GENERAL)

SB   PLANT CULTURE AND HORTICULTURE
    403-450   FLOWERS AND FLOWER CULTURE.
          ORNAMENTAL PLANTS.
        403   Periodicals and societies.
        403.Z5 History, etc. of horticulture societies, garden
               clubs, etc.
        404   Florists' directories.
             .A3, General.
             .A5-Z, By country.
             General.
        405   American.
        406   Other.
        407   Illustrations and descriptions of choice plants.
        408   Lists of ornamental plants.
              Culture of individual plants.
        409   Orchids.
        411   Roses.
        413   Other plants, A-Z.
               e.g. .A7, Aster; .A9, Azalea; .B4, Begonia;
                .C18, Camellia; .C3, Carnation; .C55,
                Chrysanthemum; etc.

CALL NUMBERS

As in the case of books classified by the Dewey Decimal Classification, it is necessary to use a book number in the call number to distinguish books in the same class number and by the same author. Compared with the numbers from the Cutter tables, the Library of Congress book numbers are very short. The arrangement is generally alphabetical by author and title. For instance, Daniel J. Foley's book *Garden Flowers in Color* would have the call number $\frac{SB405}{.F77}$; Norman Taylor's

The Guide to Garden Flowers would have the call number

$\frac{SB405}{.T3}$. The Dewey Decimal Classification class number for

Foley's book would be 635.9 and the book number would be F69g; the Dewey class number for Taylor's book would be 635.9 and the book number T216g. As illustrated by the examples under the class number SB413, the same plan may be used to keep subjects, biographees, countries, etc., in alphabetical order under a single class number. For example, Hume's book *Azaleas and Camellias* has the call number

$\dfrac{\text{SB413}}{.\text{A9}}$; his *Azaleas, Kinds and Culture,* $\dfrac{\text{SB413}}{.\text{A9}}$; his *Camellias*
$\overline{\text{H8}}$ $\overline{\text{H82}}$

in America, $\dfrac{\text{SB413}}{.\text{C18}}$.
  $\overline{\text{H8}}$

When the Library of Congress Classification is used, the numbers before the decimal point are read in ordinary sequence, but after the decimal point, they are read decimally and not as whole numbers. For instance, $\dfrac{\text{SB13}}{.\text{H3}}$ would come

before $\dfrac{\text{SB103}}{.\text{H3}}$; but $\dfrac{\text{SB411}}{.\text{P262}}$ would stand before $\dfrac{\text{SB411}}{.\text{P34}}$ on the

shelf since the two books with the same class number, SB411, would have to be arranged by the number after the decimal point.

THE
CARD
CATALOG

Student: "Have you any books on Space Flight?"
Library Assistant: "If we have, they are listed in
the card catalog."

Some students are unfamiliar with a card catalog because they have not had to use one in high school, where the books were on open shelves around the walls of the library room or in open stacks in one section of the room. Any catalog there was small compared to a university library catalog.

Many university and college libraries have their collection in closed stacks where only faculty and graduate students are allowed to work. The only key to such a collection is the card catalog. The present trend, however, in libraries of recent construction is *open* stacks where each person, faculty or student, goes for his books; everyone has direct access to the books, magazines and newspapers, pamphlets, and so on.

Even with such an arrangement, you are still dependent upon the card catalog to find out what the library has, where to find it, and how to locate it. Wandering around among thousands of books looking for the ones you need or want isn't intelligent!

INDEX TO THE BOOK COLLECTION

The card catalog is an alphabetical index to the books in the library. It is a guide to the book collection just as an index to a book is a guide to its contents. Having the index on cards makes it more convenient for use and for inserting cards for new books. The cards are filed in trays in one straight alphabetical arrangement. The printed ones are bought from the Library of Congress; the typewritten ones are prepared in your library. The label on the outside of each tray of the catalog cabinet indicates the part of the alphabet that it holds.

GUIDE CARDS

At intervals through the catalog are *guide* cards, which stand up higher than the other cards. These indicate where to *begin looking* in the tray and are great time-savers.

ALPHABETICAL ARRANGEMENT

Every book except literature (fiction, poetry, drama, essays, and so forth) *usually* has at least three cards in the catalog so that you may locate it by looking under the *author,* the *title,* or the *subject.* Obviously, these cards are filed separately wherever they belong in the alphabet. Alphabetical filing is by the first word—not an article (*a, the, an,* or their equivalents in foreign languages), at the top of the card. Some filing practices are common to most libraries. For instance, author cards for books by the same author are filed alphabetically by the words in the title, which appears immediately below the author's name. "See also" references appear *after* all cards on a subject, leading to additional information on related subjects. Abbreviations are filed as if spelled out—*Saint* for *St., Mister* for *Mr.,* and *Mac* for *Mc.* The German *umlaut* is filed as *oe* for *ö* and *ue* for *ü.*

Other variations in alphabetizing are the *word by word* method and the *letter by letter* method. This means that subject headings, authors' names, and titles of more than one word may be arranged in the alphabet by considering each word separately or by considering all of the words together as one long word. For example:

Word by Word	*Letter by Letter*
House	House
House ant	House ant
House fly	Housebreaking
House industry	House fly

Housebreaking	Household
Household	Household troops
Household troops	House industry
Houses	Houses

Usually, card catalogs are alphabetized *word by word*.

The filing code or rules for the individual library must be consulted in a great many situations where variations are possible and acceptable. In filing the cards for a number of different *editions* of a book, some libraries place the latest edition ahead of all others. The subject cards for books on the history of a country are usually filed chronologically. The rule for hyphenated words often upsets the filing code of a library because of variations used by authors of books—for instance, *root crops* and *root-crops*.

Identical names are usually filed by dates:

> Jones, John Paul, 1747–1792.
> Jones, John Paul, 1897–

Numerals in the names of royalty are filed numerically:

> Edward I, King of England, 1239–1307.
> Edward II, King of England, 1284–1327.

Punctuation marks are disregarded, as are titles of honor.

Study carefully any "stamped" information on a card. It may indicate the location of a book or call attention to the *main entry* card (usually the author card or its substitute). Always ask for information if your search leads you to a *temporary* card in the catalog—a card of another color, usually "riding the rod." It probably means that the regular cards have been removed from the catalog for revision. It does not necessarily indicate that the book is not available; so inform yourself as to the temporary-card system in your library.

CATALOG CARDS

Close attention to the catalog card will help you decide whether the book it represents is the one you want. It gives the author and title and indicates whether the book is written by one or more persons. For nonfiction it mentions the edition, if other than the first. Usually it gives the *imprint* of the book— where it was published, the name of the publisher, and the date of publication. Noticing the number of pages in the book or the number of volumes is important; if it is one of a set of books, be sure to add the number of the desired volume to the call number when requesting it or looking for it in an open-stack library. If the book is illustrated, the card will show it. Frequently, explanatory notes appear on the card—a very useful one being that noting a bibliography in the book. Then, near the bottom, the *subjects* of the book are listed, as well as an indication of other cards in the catalog for the same book. Since the card is printed at the Library of Congress, it gives the copyright number of the book, the order number for the card, the Library of Congress Classification number, and the Dewey Decimal Classification number—most of these last-mentioned items have no importance to the average catalog user.

The catalog card illustrated is typical of thousands found in most card catalogs, giving the author's full name, his date of birth (and, if not living, his date of death), the preliminary paging of the book, and so forth. Some of this information is not currently being listed on catalog cards, as shown by the following cards.

323.354 **Smith, Thomas Lynn,** 1903–
Sm6s2   The sociology of rural life. Rev. ed. By T. Lynn Smith.
New York and London, Harper & brothers ₍1947₎

xxii, 634 p. illus. (maps) plates, diagrs. 22 cm. ₍Harper's social
science series₎

Bibliography : p. 579-619.

1. Sociology, Rural. 2. Social problems. 3. Farm life.   ɪ. Title.

HT421.S55   1947   323.354   47—1364

Library of Congress   ₍57m1₎

The Physics

of Satellite Motion

Orbital
Space
Flight

Howard S. Seifert

Mary Harris Seifert

 Holt, Rinehart and Winston, Inc., New York

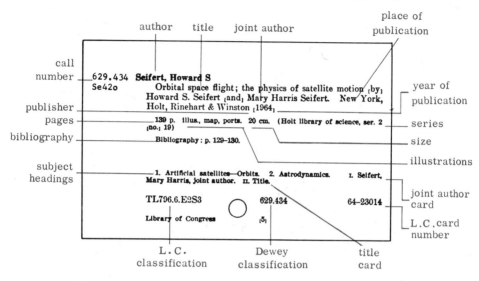

AUTHOR CARDS

To find a book by Howard S. Seifert, look under his *last name*, Seifert, for *Seifert, Howard S.*, which is the first line at the top of the card. The catalog lists those of his books that the library owns, each represented by a separate card.

If the library has more than one book by an author, the author cards are filed alphabetically by the words in the title, which appears just below the author's name. Books are listed under the author's real name, with a cross reference from his *pseudonym* (fictitious name under which he writes) if he has one.

In looking for a book by a person whose last name begins with *Mc* or *M'*, remember that it is filed as if spelled *Mac*. The same is true of *St.* and *Saint*.

JOINT AUTHORS

If more than one person writes a book, the main author card is under the author first mentioned on the title page of the book; another card is filed in the catalog for each *joint author*, whose name is typed above the main author's name.

CORPORATE ENTRIES

The government, an institution, an association, a society, or a corporation may be considered the author of a publication issued in its name. Such name, instead of a person's name, appears in the author's place on the catalog card, and it is called a *corporate entry*. For instance:

U.S. Dept. of Agriculture
American Red Cross
New York (State) Dept. of Health
Society of Arts and Sciences, New York

TITLE CARDS

Most people remember the titles of books instead of the authors. A card with the title of the book at the top (above the author's name) is filed in the catalog under the first word of the title. An article (*a, an, the,* or the foreign equivalent) is never considered the first word of a title in filing. Thus, *The art of learning* is filed under the word *art*.

The title card is *exactly* like the author card except that the title has been typed above the author's name, so that it may be filed in the correct alphabetical place for people looking for the book by its title.

                    Orbital space flight

629.434   **Seifert, Howard S**
Se420   Orbital space flight; the physics of satellite motion [by]
            Howard S. Seifert [and] Mary Harris Seifert.   New York,
            Holt, Rinehart & Winston [1964]

                 139 p. illus., map, ports. 20 cm. (Holt library of science, ser. 2
            [no.] 19)

                 Bibliography : p. 129-130.

                 1. Artificial satellites—Orbits.   2. Astrodynamics.   I. Seifert,
            Mary Harris, joint author. II. Title.

            TL796.6.E2S3   629.434   64-23014

            Library of Congress   [5]

Titles that contain numerals are filed as though the figures were written out: *One hundred million guinea pigs*, instead of *100,000,000 guinea pigs*. Rarely does a card catalog contain a title card for a biography whose title begins with the name of the person about whom the book is written—that is, *Andrew Jackson, the border captain*, by Marquis James. Generally the *subject* card suffices—listing the title under *Jackson, Andrew, pres., U.S., 1767–1845*. This is also true of books whose titles begin with *The Life of . . .* or *The History of . . . .*

Initials standing for names of organizations, and so forth, *when in titles*, are filed as initials and not as if spelled out. However, *Mr.* and *Mrs.* are filed as though spelled out, *Mister* and *Mistress*.

SUBJECT CARDS

Often you will need material on a subject without knowing any authors or titles to consult. In that case, look under the *subject itself*. Be specific, not general, in looking up subject headings. For instance, look for *Cattle*, not *Animal Husbandry*. These headings are typed in red on the top line of the subject card (above the author's name, just as on the title card). Otherwise, this card is *exactly* like the author card.

Some libraries type the subject headings in black capital letters instead of red letters. This practice prevents confusion in the mind of the user when cards for government documents are filed in the main card catalog. Cards for United States documents are prepared by the Suprintendent of Documents; the subject cards are made with black "caps" (capital letters throughout).

Some libraries have a separate catalog for government publications or documents in the Documents Department and no cards for such publications in the central or general catalog.

If the library has more than one book on a subject, all of the subject cards are together in the catalog, arranged alphabetically by the author's last name. For example: A subject card for a book on *Dance music* by Gertrude *Colby* will come before the one by Grace *Ryan*, which will come before one by Helen *Smith*.

```
                    Artificial satellites ———— Orbits

629.434   Seifert, Howard S
Se420          Orbital space flight; the physics of satellite motion ₍by₎
          Howard S. Seifert ₍and₎ Mary Harris Seifert.  New York,
          Holt, Rinehart & Winston ₍1964₎
               139 p.  illus., map, ports.  20 cm.  (Holt library of science, ser. 2
          ₍no.₎ 19)
               Bibliography: p. 129–130.



               1. Artificial satellites—Orbits.   2. Astrodynamics.       ɪ. Seifert,
          Mary Harris, joint author.  ɪɪ. Title.

          TL796.6.E2S3                         629.434                64–23014

          Library of Congress           ◯        ₍5₎
```

SUBDIVIDED SUBJECT HEADINGS

Many subjects have *subdivisions*. They are arranged alphabetically in the catalog after the general subject heading:

Mexico
Mexico—Antiquities.
Mexico—Antiquities—Bibliography.
Mexico—Bibliography.
Mexico—Bibliography—Periodicals.
Mexico—Boundaries—Guatemala.
Mexico—Boundaries—U.S.
Mexico—Church history.
Mexico—Politics and government.
Mexico—Politics and government—1910–1946.
Mexico—Social life and customs.

INVERTED SUBJECTS

Some *phrase* subject headings (more than one word) are
inverted to bring out the important word first; that is, *Photography, Aerial;* or *Photography, Commercial.* If the subject
heading you are looking for cannot be found, look under a
similar one. In most libraries, books on *World War I* are entered in the catalog under *European War 1914-1918* (in red),
with a cross reference from *World War I, 1914-1918;* but
World War II is treated under *World War, 1939-1945.*

SERIES CARDS

There are many books published as volumes in a *series*: for instance, *Great Rivers of America* and *The Reference Shelf*. There are cards in the catalog under the name of the *series*, listing the library holdings by volume and number of the series. Then, there are author, title, and subject cards in the catalog for individual volumes in the series.

```
302        The Reference shelf.                    (Card 54
R25r
           v.28,no.3    Baird, A. C.  Representative
                        American speeches.  c1956.

           v.28,no.4    Marx, H. L.  Community planning...
                        c1956.

           v.28,no.5    Daniels, W. M.  The Government and
                        the farmer.  c1956.

           v.28,no.6    McClellan, G. S.  The Middle East
                        in the cold war.  c1956.

                              ◯
```

```
302        Marx, Herbert L          ed.
R25r            Community planning.  New York, H. W. Wilson Co.,
v.28       1956.
no. 4          207 p.  21 cm.  (The Reference shelf, v. 28, no. 4)
               Bibliography : p. ₍198₎-207.



               1. Cities and towns—Planning—U. S.   I. Title.   (Series)
           NA9108.M3              711                     56-7645
           Library of Congress       ₍80₎
```

ANALYTICAL CARDS

Some libraries "analyze" the contents of a book of short stories, essays, or plays by different authors and prepare author and title cards for each one. *Subject analytics* are also prepared in some libraries for books whose chapters cover different subjects; a subject card is made for each *part* of the book dealing with a distinct subject. These *analytical cards* make each part of the book available to the users of the card catalog.

PERIODICALS

Periodicals subscribed to by the library are represented in the card catalog under the title of the periodical. Some smaller libraries place immediately in back of this card a *checklist* card showing the volumes owned by the library. However, the large libraries are discontinuing such a practice because of the immense cost of keeping this record up to date.

```
720.5     Better homes and gardens. v. 1-
B46          July 1922-
             [Des Moines, E. T. Meredith, etc., 1922

                 v. illus. 30½ cm. monthly.

          Title varies: July 1922-July 1924, Fruit, garden and home.
             Aug. 1924-              Better homes and gardens.
          Editor: July 1922-              C. C. Sherlock.



             1. Gardening—Period.  2. Fruit-culture—Period.  3. Architecture,
          Domestic—Period.   I. Sherlock, Chesla Clella, 1895-1938, ed.  II.
          Fruit, garden and home.

          NA7100.B45                                    27—6944
          Library of Congress            [58e1]
```

SIGNPOSTS

Since it is impractical to file cards under every synonym of a given subject, cross references are provided to lead to the subject under which you will find the material for which you are looking.

```
        Mardi Gras

    see

  Carnival




                          ◯

```

"See also" reference cards appear at the *end* of all cards on a *subject* (ahead of the cards for subdivisions of the subject) to lead to *additional* information on related subjects.

Photography

   see also

Astronomical photography; Cameras; Color photography; Lantern slides; Microphotography.

Name cross references have already been mentioned in connection with pseudonyms. (See p. 24) Such a card is illustrated below.

```
        Twain, Mark,

    see

  Clemens, Samuel Langhorne, 1835-1910




                          ◯

```

CALL NUMBERS

Every catalog card has the *call number* of the book in the upper left corner. In some libraries with electric charging machines this group of numbers is the only information from the catalog necessary for borrowing a book, and must be copied *accurately* on a slip of paper and presented at the Circulation Desk. Many libraries require your filling out a *call slip*, giving, in addition to the call number, the author and title of the book and your name and address. This slip becomes part of the Circulation Department records, and is also required in some libraries that have an electric "charging" machine.

It is wise, even in open-stack libraries, to fill out a call slip. If you cannot find the book on the shelf, it may be charged out to someone else, may be misshelved, or may be lost. In such instances, the Circulation Department needs the call slip to trace the book.

REFERENCE
BOOKS

Reference books have been mentioned several times in the preceding chapters; since the rest of this booklet, as well as your work in the library, is devoted to them, it may be wise to find out more about their characteristics. From our point of view, all books fall into two classes—those read for fun or for information and those consulted for a definite fact or piece of information. The latter are *reference books*. Of course, many more exist than can be treated here individually; but through the use of the library and with the Reference Librarian's help, you will learn to know them and find them useful.

Encyclopedias can and should be used for an introductory, general survey of a subject. In a large library, however, reference books in special fields should be known and employed. Finding a set of encyclopedias on the reference shelf may be like meeting an old friend, but knowing how to use it is no reason for limiting your investigation to what it can offer.

Haphazard use of reference books wastes more time during the average college career than anything else, unless we consider the Student Union! Unskillful searching frequently ends in failure unless a streak of sheer luck intervenes. Remembering the main points about these books through use is far more important than finding the answers to the practice work. Once the main points are learned, selecting the proper book for a particular question will be easy. Attention to the following items should build up an automatic technique for the use of reference books.

DATE

The date of a book is of first importance in locating information. For recent developments like radar, up-to-date reference books are necessary. In securing the latest edition of a book, remember that the "copyright" date on the back of the title page is your clue—not the date at the bottom of the title page. (See p. 9)

SUBJECTS COVERED

If you are not familiar with the scope of a reference book, look through the introduction and table of contents to see what it includes. Think of the freshman who was earnestly thumbing through the current *Who's Who in America* for the life of George Washington. His technique was faulty in three respects: The book includes only living Americans (notice the title); and the fact that its items are alphabetically arranged makes thumbing unnecessary. The *date* was wrong, to begin with.

ARRANGEMENT

The articles in most reference books are alphabetically arranged for the quick, easy location of material. If they are not so arranged, an alphabetical approach to the contents is provided—an index. However, many alphabetical books also have indexes, because the information is grouped under large subjects, and the index is the key to small subjects treated as sub-topics under the large ones.

The arrangement depends somewhat on the type of reference material being presented. In some fields, it is more advantageous to present information in a classified arrangement or in pertinent chapters. In such instances, a full index is necessary.

If the book itself does not have a key to abbreviations used in it, their meanings can be found in a dictionary.

The Best Type of Reference Book

BIBLIOGRAPHIES

The best types of reference books include *bibliographies, signed articles, and cross references.* An article in a reference book is sometimes sufficient for the needs of the average person, but often it is not. A list of books (bibliography) at the end of an important article lead to further and more intensive reading on the subject. You don't have to be a research worker to realize the value of such bibliographies.

AUTHORITY

People who write articles for reference books are usually experts and specialists, and the best type of reference book gives the author's name at the end of each important article. Some give it in full; others give initials, for which identification may be made in the list of contributors in the front. Obviously, this labeling lends authority to a book.

CROSS REFERENCES

Cross references have as much value in books as in card catalogs. An article cannot appear under every synonymous subject name. Therefore, it is entered under the one most people will think of, with cross references to it under the others. *See also* references help by leading to added information. If you do not find cross references, don't assume that the book contains nothing on your subject. Look under as many synonymous subject titles as you can think of.

CARE

Reference books are very expensive public property and must be handled by many people; they should be used with care. Putting pencil marks in them, turning down the corners of pages, or rumpling the pages is highly inconsiderate of other readers. Dropping the books may damage them a great deal.

Mutilation of books, reference books, magazines, and other library materials is a serious problem. Proper care of such materials is the responsibility of every individual. It is inconceivable that any person mature enough to use a university or college library would indulge in such childish and delinquent tendencies.

INDEXES

Magazine Indexes

Magazines contain much information that never appears in books or that is too recent to have been published in book form. So do newspapers. Some magazines are published every week, some every month, and others every two or three months. A certain number of these issues, usually covering six months, makes up a *volume;* the number of issues in a volume varies with different magazines. When a volume is complete, most libraries have it *bound* like a book, with an index to each volume.

Searching for information through the indexes in individual volumes of magazines would be a colossal task, taking more time than most people can spare. It would be like going to the shelves and searching among 200,000 books to determine whether or not the library has the one you need. *An index to magazine material is just as necessary as an index to the book collection (card catalog).* Through magazine indexes you may find articles on any subject or by almost any author.

All magazine indexes are alphabetically arranged: some, by author, title, and subject like the card catalog; others, by author and subject; and still others, only by subject. Most of them are published monthly; but at intervals through the year, one issue will not only include the current month's index but will reprint *all in one alphabet* the indexes of the issues for two, three, or six months previous, so that you need to look in only one issue instead of several. This is called a *cumulation*. Once a year each index cumulates for the whole year. For our further convenience, some indexes publish a two-year or a three-year cumulation.

READERS' GUIDE

The most-used magazine index is the *Readers' Guide to Periodical Literature,* commonly called the *Readers' Guide.* Since knowing how to use it enables you to use any other magazine index, only the *Readers' Guide* will be explained in detail.

Its field is general, covering all subjects, and it indexes magazines from 1900 to the present time. Originally it included about 15 of the most popular magazines; now, more than 100. It is published twice a month except during July and August, when there is just one issue for each month. The second issue each month includes what has been published in the first one, all in one alphabet. This cumulation keeps the index up to date and prevents having to look in two issues. This is true of the three-month cumulations also. The bound yearly volume takes the place of the paper ones for twelve months.

ARRANGEMENT

The arrangement is alphabetical, articles being entered under author and subject, and under title when necessary. Each entry gives the name of the article; the author (if known); the name of the magazine in which it appeared; and the volume, pages, and exact date. For instance:

SPACE FLIGHT ────────────────────── subject

Manned flights ──────────── subdivision of subject

title of ─────── Advanced manned research: Mars,
article

Venus trips feasible by 1980. il── illustrations

name of ─────── Miss & Roc 17:75-6+ N 29 '65
magazine   vol. pages   date

For monthly periodicals, like *Holiday,* and *Science Digest,* and *National Geographic Magazine,* only the month and the year are given:

Nat Geog Mag 129:54-65 Ja '66

You have no doubt noticed that the names of some of the magazines are abbreviated. This saves space. The full names of all magazines indexed appear in the front of each issue of an index. A key to other abbreviations is also there. Many cross references, both *see* and *see also,* are used in indexes. (See p. 12)

STORIES, PLAYS, ESSAYS, POEMS

Title entries are made for stories and plays, and occasionally for essays. Titles of poems are grouped under the subject *Poems.*

WHAT TO COPY

If you want the articles you have located through the index, copy very accurately the full name of the magazine, the volume number, the date, and (for your own benefit) the inclusive pages of the article. If your library requires a call slip, your name and address must also be given, and the paging is not listed.

OTHER

Poole's Index to Periodical Literature, 1802-1907. An index to subjects only—no author entries. The ancestor of all magazine indexes, it is the only index to nineteenth-century periodicals up to 1890. *Poole* does not give the date in the entry for an article—only the volume and paging. The date can be computed from a table in the front of the index if you need it.

Nineteenth Century Readers' Guide to Periodical Literature, 1890-1899. In contrast to *Poole's Index,* this includes author and illustrator entries, as well as subject entries, and the title entries to short stories, novels, plays, and poems. Book reviews are well indexed.

Handbook of Latin American Studies. 1935-date. Annotated *index* to periodical articles and books on Latin America. Arranged by broad subject and geographical areas, then alphabetical by author under each area. In the full author index and the subject index in the back, entries refer to item numbers and not to page references. Since 1964 this index has been

READERS' GUIDE
to periodical literature

AUTHOR AND SUBJECT INDEX

February 18—March 24, 1966

ABA. See American booksellers association
ACF industries
Booms, rails and ACF. J. Weingarten. Duns R 87:49-50 Mr '66
ADP (automatic data processing) See Electronic data processing
AEC. See United States—Atomic energy commission
AGMA. See American guild of musical artists
AI. See Artificial insemination
AID. See United States—Agency for international development
AIGA. See American institute of graphic arts
ARL. See Association of research libraries
ARPA. See United States—Defense, Department of—Advanced research projects agency
ASNLH. See Association for the study of Negro life and history
ATS (applications technology satellites) See Artificial satellites
AWACS (airborne warning and control system) See Radar defense network
ABDUCTION. See Kidnaping
ABDUCTION from the seraglio; opera. See Mozart, J. C. W. A.
ABILITY
Balancing ability with humility; interview. S. J. Weinberg. il Nations Bsns 53:44-6+ D '65
Examination of transfer of learning by nucleic acid. M. Luttges and others. bibliog il Science 151:834-7 F 18 '66
ABILITY, Influence of age on
Visually evoked potentials: amplitude changes with age. R. E. Dustman and E. C. Beck. bibliog il Science 151:1013-15 F 25 '66
ABILITY tests
Diagnosis, retarded. P. Deutsch and R. Deutsch. il Parents Mag 41:56-7+ Mr '66
ABLATION shielding. See Shielding (heat)
ABORTION
Abortion laws. Commonweal 83:685 Mr 18 '66
ABSORPTION spectra
Studies of alloys by X-ray absorption spectroscopy. L. V. Azároff. bibliog il Science 151:785-9 F 18 '66
ACADEMIC freedom
Academic freedom and political liberty. A. Lepawsky; reply. S. K. Escalona. Science 151:1034 Mr 4 '66
Battle for your child's mind. R. D. Batchelder. Parents Mag 41:40+ Mr '66
St John's university: the issues. F. Canavan; discussion. America 114:241, 276-7 F 19-26 '66
Strike at St John's. J. Leo. Commonweal 83:500+ Ja 28 '66; Reply. S. Poole. 83:705 Mr 18 '66
See also
Colleges and universities—Political control
ACADEMIES (schools) See Private schools
ACADIANS in Louisiana
Cajunland, Louisiana's French-speaking coast. B. Keating. il Nat Geog Mag 129:352-91 Mr '66
ACARINA. See Mites
ACCELERATORS (electrons, etc)
Beam storage in the Cambridge electron accelerator; letter. M. S. Livingston. Science 151:936 F 25 '66
ACCELEROMETERS
Accelerometer calibration simplified. Miss & Roc 18:45 F 28 '66
ACCIDENT benefit plans. See Employees benefit plans
ACCIDENTS, Industrial
Statistics
Work injuries; tables. See issues of Monthly labor review

ACCOUNTABILITY (law)
See also
Criminal liability
ACCREDITATION of public schools. See Public schools—Accreditation
ACCULTURATION
Sell-out or the well acculturated Christian. R. E. Fitch. Christian Cent 83:202-5 F 16 '66; Discussion. 83:370-2 Mr 23 '66 .
ACE books, incorporated
Ace books reaches agreement with Tolkien. Pub W 189:37-8 Mr 14 '66
ACOUSTICS, Architectural
How to shop for a silent ceiling. il Bet Hom & Gard 44:133 Mr '66
Sound and the fury. R. W. Hall. il Opera N 30:8-13 Mr 26 '66
ACQUISITIONS, Library. See Libraries—Acquisitions
ACROBATICS, Aerial. See Aviation—Stunt flying
ACRONYMS
FASGROLIA; fast growing language of initialisms and acronyms. Newsweek 67:94+ Mr 14 '66
ACRYLAMIDE
Acrylamide-gel electrophorograms by mechanical fractionation; radioactive adenovirus proteins. J. V. Maizel, jr. bibliog il Science 151:988-90 F 25 '66
ACTING
Face to face: with a dresser with dreams. L. Saroyan. Seventeen 25:137 F '66
Reflections of a secret soldier of fortune; ed. by E. Miller. R. Redford. Seventeen 25:126-7+ F '66
See also
Improvisation (acting)
ACTINOMYCIN
Actinomycin D: inhibition of respiration and glycolysis. J. Laszlo and others. bibliog il Science 151:1007-10 F 25 '66
ACTIONS and defenses
Anecdotes, facetiae, satire, etc.
Look at the spring suits. F. P. Tullius. New Yorker 42:86+ F 26 '66
ACTORS and actresses
Imports. L. Lerman. il Mlle 62:156-9 F '66
ADAM, Adolphe Charles
Le diable à quatre. G. L. Mayer. il Am Rec G 32:591 Mr '66
ADAMO, S. J.
Yearling. America 114:336 Mr 5 '66
ADAMS, Bert N.
How Bert beat the bureaucrats. por Time 87:61 Mr 4 '66
ADAMS, Junius
Some thoughts on the meaning of life; story. Esquire 65:90-3 F '66
ADAMS, Philip R.
Some thoughts on the environmental arts. Antiques 89:391-408 Mr '66
ADAMS, Ruth Marie
New name on Wellesley's door. por Time 87:70 Mr 25 '66
ADAPTATION, Social. See Adjustment, Social
ADARKAR, Vivek B.
Girl as pretty as the Taj; story. Seventeen 25:124-5 F '66
ADDICTS, Drug. See Narcotic addicts
ADEN
Will Britain's loss be Nasser's gain? il U S News 60:91-3 Mr 28 '66
ADENOVIRUSES
Acrylamide-gel electrophorograms by mechanical fractionation; radioactive adenovirus proteins. J. V. Maizel, jr. bibliog il Science 151:988-90 F 25 '66
ADIRONDACK MOUNTAINS
Adirondack trails; reprint. P. Schaeffer. Liv Wildn 29:36-7 Aut '65

EXPLANATION

Sample title: Cajunland, Louisiana's French-speaking coast. B. Keating. il Nat Geog Mag 129:352-91 Mr '66

Explanation: An article with the title given, written by B. (Bern) Keating, can be found in National Geographic Magazine, volume 129, pages 352-391, the March 1966 issue.

SELECTED REFERENCES FROM THE READERS' GUIDE

December 10, 1965, January 25, 1966, February 10, 1966

ALSTON, Ralph E. See Melchert, T. E. jt. ——— Joint author reference
auth.

AMERICAN medical association
Colds, gout, overweight: what's new; meeting. US ——— Official or society
News 59:12 D 13 '65   author

DRAMA
       Study and teaching ——— Subheading under
Bruner on drama; excerpts from address, July 1965,   Drama
  Sr Schol 87:sup 12 D 2 '65
  See also ——— See also reference
Dramatization in education
       Themes
Father's day on Broadway. T. Frideaux. il Life 59:
  72A-72B N 5 '65

                                  Inverted subject
DRAMA, Medieval ——— heading
Heigh, Sir Ass, oh heigh; Play of Daniel and the
  Play of Herod. F. Bowers. il House & Gard 128:
  183-4+ D '65 ——— Illustrations

DRAMAS
There's some milk in the icebox. B. J. Henderson.
  il Mlle 62:176-7+ N '65
  See also ——— See also reference
Detective and mystery plays
Fairy plays
       Criticisms, plots, etc. ——— Subheading under
Theater (cont) Nat R 17:561-2, 660; 18:37-9 Je 29, Drama
  Jl 27 '65. Ja 11 '66
  See also ——— Article continued in
London—Theater several numbers
      single works
    See name of author for full entry
Cactus flower. A. Burrows General articles first,
Country wife. W. Wycherley then see reference to
Herakles. A. MacLeish author's name for single
Les joies de la famille. See Very rich woman, below works
Malcolm, E. Albee
Very rich woman. R. Gordon
You can't take it with you. M. Hart and G. S. Kauf-
  man

FRENAYE, Frances
  (tr) See Bodin, S. Bettina: the adventures of a ——— Translator reference
  passionate traveller

JOHNSON, Lady Bird. See Johnson, C. A. T. ——— See reference to real
  name

LONG, Edward V.
  Speaking out. por Sat Eve Post 238:10+ N 20 '65
LONG, Russell Billiu ——— Portrait
Excerpt from address, September 15, 1965. Cong
  Digest 44:268+ N '65
Growing power for Louisiana's Long. por US News
  59:20 N 29 '65 If author and subject
    same word, author
LONG ISLAND daily listed first
Letters from Steinbeck; H. F. Guggenheim hires J.
  Steinbeck. Newsweek 66:68 N 22 '65

LONG playing record catalog. See Phonograph
  records—Catalogs ——— See reference

MADAME Butterfly: opera. See Puccini, G.

MISSILE sleds. See Rocket sleds ——————————— See reference

MOVING picture plays
  See also

    Criticisms, plots, etc.
  SR's annual survey of the movies; symposium. il Sat
    R 48:10-22+ D 25 '65
  Spotlight! E. Miller. See issues of Seventeen be-
    ginning April 1965

       Single works
  Agony and the ecstasy
    Christian Cent 82:1548 D 15 '65
  Bedford incident
    Sat R 48:75 D 4 '65
  Doctor Zhivago
    Esquire 64:132+ D '65
  Patch of blue
    Commonweal 83:376 D 24 '65
    Time 86:98+ D 17 '65

Moving picture plays;
general articles first,
then alphabetical by
title under <u>single</u>
works

MUSIC writing. See Composition (music)

RUSK, Dean
  Excerpt from testimony, July 30, 1965. Cong Digest
    44:300+ D '65
  Rusk to Hanoi: no Vietnam backdown; excerpts
    from interview. U S News 59:10 D 20 '65
  Secretary Rusk's news conference:
    November 5, 1965. Dept. State Bul 53:854-62 N 29
    '65
  Unseen search for peace; address, October 16, 1965.
    Vital Speeches 32:66-71 N 15 '65

       about
  Credibility of commitment. il Time 86:9 D 24 '65
  What liberty means. il por Newsweek 66:26 N 29 '65

Titles in two alphabets:
articles <u>by</u>,
then articles <u>about</u>

SENTER, Raymond D pseud. ——————————— Pseudonym
  Nuclear weapons in orbit. New Repub 153:11-12 N
    27 '65; 154:36 Ja 1 '66 ——————————— Continued article

See reference to
  author's name for
  information

SMALL miracle; story. See Gallico, P. ——————————

SPACE vehicles

Subdivision of
  subject

    Landing systems
      Moon
  Three giant steps to the moon. il Pop Mech 124: ——Continued article
    90-4+ O; 116-20+ N; 104-8+ D '65

divided into two parts, appearing in alternate years: (1) Humanities, (2) Social Sciences.

Index to Latin American Periodical Literature, 1929-1960. 8 vols. Prepared by the Pan American Union. Primarily in the fields of economics, politics, government, and social and cultural fields. Arrangement is by author, subject, and other secondary entries. Continued by the following index.

Index to Latin American Periodicals; Humanities and Social Sciences. 1961-1962. 2 vols. Dictionary arrangement, with authors, titles, and subjects all in one alphabet. Many cross references. Accompanied by useful lists. It is now a quarterly index, alphabetical by subject with an author index. Annual cumulation.

Canadian Periodical Index, 1948-date, is another useful index.

Ulrich's International Periodicals Directory. 1965–1966. 11th ed. Not an index, but complements all of them. A selected list of foreign and domestic periodicals. Vol. 1 covers scientific, technical, and medical fields. Vol. 2 covers the fields of the arts, humanities, business, and social sciences. The arrangement is by classified subjects and in the back is a detailed subject index (key to subjects), as well as two appendixes.

Magazine and Other Indexes in Special Fields

BIOGRAPHY

Biography Index. 1946-date. A one-place index to biographical material in magazines and in books, universal in scope. It has two sections—an alphabetical name index, and an index to professions and occupations, alphabetical by subject. Published quarterly with an annual volume in August.

BUSINESS AND PUBLIC AFFAIRS

Business Periodicals Index. 1958-date. Cumulative *subject* index to periodicals in the fields of accounting, advertising, banking and finance, general business, labor and management, insurance, public administration, taxation, specific businesses, and industries and trades. Published monthly except July; annual cumulation. Formerly part of *Industrial Arts Index.*

Public Affairs Information Service. Bulletin. 1915-date. A *subject* index in the fields of sociology, economics, and political science—from the practical side particularly. Indexes not only periodicals, but books, documents, pamphlets, and reports of public and private agencies relating to economic and social conditions, public administration, and international relations published in English throughout the world. Commonly called P.A.I.S.

Published weekly from September through July, fortnightly during August. Cumulates five times yearly, the fifth being the annual volume.

SCIENCE AND TECHNOLOGY

Applied Science and Technology Index. 1958-date. Cumulative *subject* index to periodicals in the fields of aeronautics, automation, chemistry, construction, electricity and electrical communication, engineering, geology and metallurgy, industrial and mechanical arts, physics, transportation, and related subjects. Published monthly except August; annual cumulation. Formerly part of the *Industrial Arts Index.*

Biological and Agricultural Index. 1916-date. Formerly the *Agricultural Index,* name changed in September, 1964. Now limited to periodicals, this cumulative *subject* index covers the fields of biology, agriculture, and related subjects, with a fairly equal division between the two sciences. Monthly, except September; cumulates quarterly, then every two years.

Engineering Index. 1906-date. Indexes material from technological magazines, bulletins, and documents, giving abstracts of the articles. Some recently published books are indexed also. In two parts: annotated subject index with full information, followed by an author index which gives only the page reference to entries in the subject index. Annual through 1961, it is now published monthly with an annual cumulation in two volumes, with an author index in the back of the second volume.

Industrial Arts Index. 1913-1957. A *subject* index to magazine articles, pamphlets, and books on engineering, trade, business, and finance. In January 1958 this index was divided into two separate publications: the *Applied Science and Technology Index* and the *Business Periodicals Index.*

A Guide to Information in Space Science and Technology. c1963. Arranged by subject with annotated entries alphabetical by author under each field. This guide exploits selective current sources, both published and unpublished. In the back are useful appendixes, followed by a detailed author index, title index, and serial publications index.

It is volume 1 of *Guides to Information Sources in Science and Technology*. Subsequent guides will cover the fields of atomic energy, biochemistry, biophysics, agriculture, biology, meteorology, geology and minerals, earth sciences, electronics, engineering, etc. Annual or biennial follow-up volumes will be published for most of the guides in the series.

Another helpful one is *Guide to the Literature of Mathematics and Physics; Including Related Works on Engineering Sciences*, c1958.

Cumulated Index Medicus. 1960-date. Indexes approximately 6,000 journals of medicine and science. Supersedes *Current List of Medical Literature* and *Quarterly Cumulated Index Medicus*, 1927-1959. In two sections: subject index and name index. Published monthly, cumulates annually. The monthly issues carry a bibliography of medical reviews and are called *Index Medicus*.

SOCIAL SCIENCES

Social Sciences and Humanities Index. 1907-date. The title and content of this index have changed from time to time: 1907-March 1955, *International Index to Periodicals;* 1955-March 1957, *International Index, A Guide to Periodical Literature in Social Science and Humanities;* 1957-June 1965, *International Index, A Quarterly Guide to Periodical Literature in the Social Sciences and Humanities*.

Beginning in June, 1955, scientific, psychological, and foreign-language periodicals were dropped. It is now an author and subject index to the more scholarly journals in the social sciences and the humanities, international in scope. Published in June, September, and December, formerly with an annual cumulation in March. From April, 1958 to April, 1964 cumulations were published every two years; however, beginning in April, 1964, annual cumulations are published.

Another useful publication is *Sources of Information in the Social Sciences; A Guide to the Literature*, c1964. Author and title index.

Education Index. 1929-date. An author and subject index to educational literature, including magazines, books, pamphlets, reports, and so forth. Published monthly, except in July and August. Cumulates four times yearly, with annual and biennial volumes in June.

Research Studies in Education; A Subject Index to Doctoral Dissertations, Reports and Field Studies with two cumulations: 1941-1952 and 1953-1963. Annual between cumulations. Alphabetical by categories, then by author under each category.

Educational Media Index. c1964. 14 vols. Each volume covers a different subject, with a title index in the back. Vol. 14 is a title index to the other 13 vols. Supplements to keep the set up to date are planned.

A *guide* to educational materials is *How To Locate Educational Information and Data*, 1958, 4th rev. ed.

FINE ARTS

ART

Art Index. 1929-date. An author and subject index to fine arts periodicals and museum bulletins. It is issued quarterly, with an annual volume in October.

Two other helpful ones are *Picture Sources*, c1964, 2nd ed., and *Illustration Index*, 1957, with a supplement for 1956-1959, published in 1961. Also useful is *Guide to Art Reference Books*, 1959, not an index to periodicals.

ARCHITECTURE

Architectural Index. 1950-date. Alphabetical subject index to selected architectural periodicals, with a full section under "Architect or Designer" in alphabetical arrangement.

Another index is *Avery Index to Architectural Periodicals*, 1963, 12 vols. Supplement, 1965.

MUSICAL AND PERFORMING ARTS

Music Index. 1949-date. Author, title, and subject index. Book reviews listed alphabetically under that subject. Cross references from titles to composers. Monthly, with an annual cumulation.

Guide to the Musical Arts; An Analytical Index of Articles and Illustrations, 1953-1956. 1957. In two parts: author and subject index to articles, and an index to illustrations.

Guide to the Performing Arts. 1957-date. This one also is in two parts: author, title, and subject index to articles on the performing arts; author, subject, and name of *TV* show index to the television arts.

Guide to Dance Periodicals. 1931-date. Biennial, with annual subject and author index.

Song Index. 1926, with a 1934 supplement. Contains titles, first lines, composers' and authors' names in one alphabet.

Index to Song Books. 1964. Indexes songs published in books between 1933 and 1962, and is intended to take up where *Song Index* left off, but is not so comprehensive or authoritative.

Speech Index; An Index to 64 Collections of World Famous Orations and Speeches for Various Occasions. 1935. Supplement, 1933-1955, and another for 1956-1961. Arranged by author, title, and type of speech, all in one alphabet. Many cross references.

LITERATURE

Four of the best indexes in the field of historical literature are: *The American Historical Association's Guide to Historical Literature,* 1961; *Guide to the Best Fiction, English and American,* 1932; *Guide to the Best Historical Fiction,* 1914; and *Guide to the Best Historical Novels and Tales,* 1929, 5th ed. These are chronologically arranged, with author and title indexes. Another fine one is *Historical Fiction Guide; Annotated, Chronological and Topical List of 5,000 Selected Historical Novels,* 1963.

Essay and General Literature Index. 1900-date. Author, subject, and title (when necessary) index to essays and articles published since 1900. It first appeared in 1934, covering 1900-1933. Since then, publication has occurred twice a year, the second issue being the annual volume. In the back is a list of books indexed, checked for the library's holdings.

Cumulated Fiction Index, 1945-1960. 1960. Almost entirely English, published in England. It began in 1953 as the *Fiction Index,* covering 1941-1953, with a supplement for 1953-1957.

The 1945-1960 volume is a revised cumulation of the two volumes of *Fiction Index,* plus coverage of material published between 1957 and 1960. Plans for another supplement are under way. Author, title, subject index all in one alphabet. In the back is an author list, alphabetical by nationality.

Short Story Index. 1953. *Supplements,* 1950-1954 and 1955-1958, the latter published in 1960. These three volumes supersede Firkin's *Index to Short Stories.* Indexed by author, title, and in many cases by subject, all in one alphabet, with full information listed under author. Pt. 2 is a list of collections, indexed by author.

Twentieth-Century Short Story Explication; Interpretations 1900-1960 Inclusive, of Short Fiction since 1800. 1961. Supplement One, 1963, covers interpretations since 1960 of short fiction since 1800. Supplement Two, 1965, covers interpretations, April 1, 1963-December 31, 1964.

These three volumes give sources of interpretation of explanation of the meaning of stories. Alphabetical by author whose stories are referred to, then alphabetical by title of story under each author. In the back is an alphabetical list of short story writers.

Dramatic Index. 1909-1949. An index to theatrical *articles* in American and English *periodicals,* covering the stage and screen. Alphabetical by subject and title. No longer published, it appeared quarterly in the *Bulletin of Bibliography* and annually with the *Magazine Subject Index.*

Index to Plays, 1800-1926; Supplement, 1927-1934. An index to many thousands of plays appearing in collections and elsewhere, arranged in two parts: an author index with full information, and then a title and subject index. In the back are two lists of *collections* of plays indexed.

Index to Full-length Plays, 1895-1925, 1956, and *Index to Full-length Plays, 1926-1944,* 1946, are two volumes of great use. Each contains three indexes—authors, titles, and subjects—with full information about each play in the title index, to which the author and subject indexes refer. The subject index is most helpful.

Index to One-Act Plays. 1958. 5 vols. The basic volume, with four supplementary volumes, covers the period from 1900 through 1957. The last two contain plays for radio, and the fifth one has plays for television, as well as for stage and radio. Alphabetical by title, with an author and subject index.

Play Index, 1949-1952. 1953. *Supplement, 1953-1960.* 1963. This index augments but does not supersede Firkins' *Index to Plays* and its supplements.

Arranged in four parts: (1) main list arranged by author, title, and subject (full information under author); (2) list of collections indexed; (3) cast analysis, a new feature listing each play under the type of cast—male, female, mixed, puppet —and number of characters; (4) directory of publishers. Indexes all types of plays, including radio and TV plays, for both children and adults.

Index to Plays in Collections, 1900-1962. 1964, 4th ed. Limited to books published in England and in the United States, this is an author and title index to plays from ancient to modern times but published between 1900 and 1962. Regular supplements are anticipated.

Granger's Index to Poetry. 1962, 5th ed. First published in 1904, this edition is completely revised and enlarged through June 30, 1960. Arrangement is in three parts: (1) title and first-line index, (2) author index, (3) subject index. Earlier editions are useful for the indexing of anthologies omitted later. The title formerly was *Index to Poetry and Recitations.*

Poetry Explication; A Checklist of Interpretation Since 1925 of British and American Poems Past and Present. 1962, rev. ed. References to interpretations are listed alphabetically by author or by works being interpreted.

RELIGION

Catholic Periodical Index. 1930-date. Prepared by the Catholic Library Association. A cumulative author and subject index to a selected list of Catholic periodicals, international in scope. Published quarterly—April and October cover three-month periods; July and December cover six months, replacing the two quarterly issues. The bound volume cumulates for two years.

Guide to Catholic Literature. 1888-date. An author, title, and subject index in one alphabet to books and pamphlets by

Catholics or of particular Catholic interest, European as well as American. Vol. 1 covers the period from 1888 to 1940. Subsequent volumes are published every four years.

Index to Religious Periodical Literature. 1949-date. Prepared by the American Theological Library Association. General index to periodical resources in the areas of religious and theological scholarship and related subjects. Basically Protestant, but includes selected Roman Catholic and Jewish journals. Ecumenical on both scholarly and popular levels; international in scope.

The first four volumes cover more than one year each; beginning in 1960 it is annual, with cumulations every three years. The arrangement is by author and subject in one alphabet. Both annual and cumulated volumes have book reviews indexed by author in the second part of the volume.

Index to Jewish Periodicals. 1963-date. Author and subject index to selected American and Anglo-Jewish journals of general and scholarly interest. In the front is a list of periodicals indexed. Quarterly, with annual (varies) cumulations.

BOOKS

Cumulative Book Index. 1929-date. A world list of books in the English language. Issued monthly except in August, it cumulates in July and in December. Periodically it cumulates for a number of years; all such volumes since 1928 are supplements of the *United States Catalog.* Alphabetically arranged by author, title, and subject.

Standard Catalog for Public Libraries . . . . 1958, 4th ed. A classified (Dewey) list of nonfiction books with an author, title, subject, and analytical index. Extremely useful for selecting some of the best books in any field, it includes comments with every title, and some full annotations. Annual supplements keep it up to date and cumulate periodically.

Fiction Catalog. 1961, 7th ed. Annotated list of fiction in the English language, with subject and title index, and also a directory of publishers of books listed. Annual supplements, not cumulative.

The Reader's Adviser. 1964. 10th ed. An annotated guide to the best in print in literature, biographies, dictionaries, encyclopedias, Bibles, classics, drama, poetry, fiction, science, philosophy, travel, and history. Full trade information given. Reference books precede the main divisions of literature. Juveniles generally omitted. Exhaustive index.

BOOK REVIEWS

Book Review Digest. 1905-date. Digested reviews of current books with references to full reviews. Issued monthly, except during February and July, it cumulates at each half-year (August) and in an annual volume in February. Alphabetical by author with a title and subject index.

The following is an example of a reference from the *Book Review Digest:*

> STONE, IRVING. The agony and the ecstasy; a
> novel of Michelangelo. 664 p. $5.95 Doubleday
>
> "Michelangelo's career is traced from his prom-
> ising boyhood . . . through all the many years
> of his flowering genius . . ."
>
> Atlantic 207:104 My '61 90 w
> Cath World 193:328 Ag '61 300 w
> N Y Times Book R p6 Mr 19 '61 700 w
> Time 77:90 Mr 24 '61 200 w

Irving Stone is the author. *The Agony and the Ecstasy; A Novel of Michelangelo* is the title of the book, 664 pages, priced at $5.95, and published by Doubleday. A brief annotation or summary of the book follows, then the condensed reviews which lead to the full reviews by giving the name of the magazine, volume, page, date, and the length of the review, for instance, 90 words.

Book Review Index. 1965-date. This index to book reviews covers a greater number and variety of periodicals indexed than does the *Book Review Digest;* however, there are no digests or annotations of the book reviews. The entries include author of the book, title, name of the periodical in which the review appears, name of the reviewer, volume, date, and paging. Alphabetical by author and a few reference book titles, but without a title and subject index. Published monthly, with quarterly cumulations.

An Index to Book Reviews in the Humanities. 1960-date. Arranged alphabetically by author or book being reviewed, followed by the code number of the periodical (numerical-alphabetical list in the front which *must* be referred to), date, and page number of the periodical where the review is to be found. Published quarterly, with an annual cumulation.

Time will be saved if the explanation in the front of the index is read. Publications of the Modern Language Association abbreviations for periodicals are used.

Technical Book Review Index. 1935-date. Identifies book reviews in current scientific, technical, and trade journals and, when feasible, quotes from them. Arranged alphabetically by author. Published monthly, except July and August, it cumulates into an annual volume with a cumulated author index.

Mathematical Reviews. 1940-date. Arranged by subject field, then alphabetical by author. It has signed reviews and an author index. Published monthly.

PUBLIC DOCUMENTS

Document Catalogue. 1893-date. The permanent, complete catalog of all U.S. government publications. It lists all documents under author, subject, and when necessary, title. Serial numbers are given for documents in the serial set. An excellent index, but it appears irregularly. The *Monthly Catalogue* keeps it up to date. All of the publications issued by government bodies since 1895 are listed here. The arrangement is alphabetical by major departments, independent institutions, and Congress. An author and subject index is published for each calendar year. It is through this index that the *Monthly Catalogue* supplements the *Document Catalogue.*

A Popular Guide to Government Publications. 1963, 2nd ed. Covers 1951-1962, for publications of the more familiar departments and agencies of the U.S. Government, but excludes reference and statistical works, laws, bibliographies, speeches, periodicals, highly technical and purely ephemeral materials. Arranged alphabetically by broad subject (listed in the table of contents). Minute subject index in the back. Many annotations.

A Guide to the Use of United Nations Documents. 1962. Includes references to the specialized agencies and special U.N. bodies. Particularly useful to political scientists, historians, economists, and other research workers in the social sciences and law. Classified arrangement by chapters. Limited index, to be used with the table of contents.

Newspaper Index

The New York Times Index. 1913-date. A subject index to *The New York Times.* From 1912 to 1929 it was published four times a year, then monthly; and now it is published twice each month, with a yearly cumulated volume. An added feature, a list of News Highlights of the Year, precedes the actual index.

Each entry gives exact reference to the day (not the year, because the index never cumulates for more than one year), page, and column; for Sunday it gives the section also:

THEATRE

    United States

        $1.25-million theatre planned, Fort Worth, Tex, financed by and named for late W E Scott, N 19, 32:1
        Tulane Drama Rev sponsors conf, NYC, on state of theatre N 22, 48:1; conf revd, N 28, II, 4:5

The first article appeared in *The New York Times* of November 19 (1965), page 32, column 1. The second article was for November 22 (1965), page 48, column 1. The third one was for November 28 (1965), section 2, page 4, column 5.

The New York Times Index does not give the *title* of the article (headline) but a summary or abstract, concise and informative. It is a day-by-day history of the world. Alphabetical word by word, under subjects and personal and organization names.

This index can be used for other newspapers for national and international news by using the *date.*

Abstracts

An abstract is a type of index. In addition to the usual information, it gives a *summary* or *abstract* of the article, book, or whatever is being indexed. As with bibliographies, many areas of important research are covered by *abstracts*. A few of the outstanding ones are:

International Aeroespace Abstracts. 1961–date.
Nuclear Science Abstracts. 1948–date.
Science Abstracts. 1898–date.
Biological Abstracts. 1926–date.
Geophysical Abstracts. 1929/1930–date.
Geological Abstracts. 1953–1959.
Geoscience Abstracts. 1959–date.
Chemical Abstracts. 1907–date.
Historical Abstracts. 1775–1945.
Sociological Abstracts. 1952–date.
Psychological Abstracts. 1927–date.
Abstracts of English Studies. 1958–date.

Bibliographies

In almost all important areas of research *bibliographies* have been published (See p. 11). A *few* of the prominent ones are:

International Bibliography of Economics. 1952–date. Annual.
International Bibliography of Political Science. 1952–date. Annual.
International Bibliography of Social and Cultural Anthropology. 1955–date. Annual.
International Bibliography of Sociology. 1951–date. Annual.
A Critical Bibliography of Religion in America. 1961. 2 vols.
A Bibliographical Guide to the History of Christianity. c1931.

Extremely useful is the *Bibliographic Index; A Cumulative Bibliography of Bibliographies.* 1937-date. Now semiannual with an annual cumulation.

DICTIONARIES

Radio, television, and movies have developed an amazing interest in pronunciation. This is due to supposedly new pronunciations. They aren't new; they are correct. Before a picture is "shot," research provides correct pronunciation. Before a program is broadcast or televised, the manuscript is carefully "edited" and rehearsed.

For generations people either mispronounce words or use other than preferred pronunciations because they never *hear* otherwise. One person relates the shock he received when he heard someone say Nū'fun(d)-land'. He had always said Nū found'land—his geography teacher in grammar school had taught him to say it that way! As a matter of fact, it never was Nū found'land. It looked that way; so his teacher didn't bother to consult the dictionary.

A dictionary gives more information about words than any other reference book—spelling, pronunciation, meaning, derivation, usage, synonyms, and antonyms. An *unabridged* dictionary includes all words in the language with all of their definitions. An *abridged* dictionary is condensed. The two most widely used unabridged American dictionaries are *Webster's New International Dictionary* and *Funk and Wagnalls New Standard Dictionary*. When you use a dictionary, remember that in the front is a full explanation of the abbreviations used, as well as a key to pronunciation symbols. The latter is given at the top or bottom of each page in some dictionaries. Unless the dictionary is a new edition or a new printing, the *addenda* should be consulted for new words added since the last printing.

AMERICAN

Webster's Third New International Dictionary. c1966. This controversial unabridged dictionary departs from many former Webster practices. To use this reference book efficiently, thorough familiarity with the introduction is necessary. The horizontally divided page has been abandoned, as well as have the gazetteer, the biographical dictionary, and synonyms for words. Abbreviations are in the main alphabet. Pronunciation is given by a newly-devised system with the key to it *only* in the introduction.

This edition presents the language as it is now *used;* therefore, much is included that may be considered colloquial, incorrect, or in bad taste. However, new scientific and technical terms are well represented.

Since the second edition, 1934, is a distinguished dictionary, with its reliability and very clear definitions, it must be included here. A heavy black line divides each page horizontally, but the amount of material below the line has been reduced to very little. It includes only very rare and out-of-date words, and long foreign phrases. Above the line are found all of the regular words in our language, foreign words, noted names in fiction, and so forth.

A number of valuable lists appear in the appendix. Some of them are: (1) abbreviations—the meaning of those in common use, (2) pronouncing biographical dictionary—brief notes about persons, (3) pronouncing gazetteer—brief descriptions of places.

If you happen to use the reprints of the second edition, remember that in the front of the book is a section called "Addenda" or "New Words," which kept each reprint up to date until the new edition was published. The second edition gives both synonyms and antonyms, and they are found at the end of the definitions for the word under SYN. and ANT. This feature is especially gratifying to persons doing any sort of writing, as it helps them to avoid too frequent use of the same words.

Webster's New Twentieth Century Dictionary. c1964. Unabridged, authoritative, up to date, and readable.

Funk and Wagnalls New Standard Dictionary of the English Language. 1963. Another unabridged dictionary. Everything in one alphabet, except foreign words and phrases, population statistics, and disputed pronunciations, which are listed in the back. Its emphasis is upon present-day meaning, pronunciation, and spelling. For this reason, it is the most useful dictionary for quick reference.

The *New Standard* gives synonyms and antonyms. The discussion of the former gives definition by *comparison,* and the latter gives definition by *contrast.* In the front is a supplement for new words since the last printing.

The Random House Dictionary of the English Language. c1966. An entirely new dictionary that reflects the explosion of knowledge in the mid-20th century, showing the growth of the language. This broad sweep of the English language includes foreign words and phrases, biographical terms, geographical terms, abbreviations, titles of major literary works, etc.

It has a high standard of scholarship combined with a balanced application of linguistics. This dictionary places great importance on communication with the user by clear and simple definitions and a good coverage of idiomatic expressions in the language. After many entries there are synonym and antonym lists, SYN. and ANT. Usage lables among definitions provide the user "with an exact record of the language he sees and hears." A concise pronunciation key is at the bottom of each odd-numbered page and a concise etymology key at the bottom of each even-numbered page.

The useful supplements in the back include four concise language dictionaries: French, Spanish, Italian, and German. Also, there is a good Atlas of the World and a gazetteer.

The Century Dictionary, in twelve volumes, borders on an encyclopedia in the fullness of its material; but a new edition has not been published since 1911. Even in this edition, the new material has been added in a supplement in the back of each volume. The *New Century Cyclopedia of Names,* three volumes, published in 1957, supersedes Volume 11 of this dictionary. Useful for identifying people and places.

There are additional, useful dictionaries for quick reference:

> *Funk and Wagnalls Standard Collegiate Dictionary.* c1963.
> *Webster's New World Dictionary of the American Language.* c1960.
> *Webster's Seventh New Collegiate Dictionary.* c1965.
> *World Book Encyclopedia Dictionary.* 1966.

ENGLISH

The Oxford English Dictionary. 1961. 13 vols. This is a corrected reissue of *Murray's New English Dictionary,* with an introduction, supplement of new words, and bibliography. It is the most scholarly dictionary of the English language, published in England. It gives the history of every English word from the middle of the twelfth century, with quotations to illustrate its use at different periods.

An additional, useful dictionary for quick reference is:

> *The Concise Dictionary of Current English.* 1964. 5th ed. Based on the *Oxford Dictionary.*

Nearly everyone has a dictionary at home, and it is the most "thumbed" book in the library; but many people do not realize how useful it can be if its different parts are known and the technique of using it is learned.

FOREIGN

> *Cassell's Italian Dictionary; Italian-English, English-Italian.* 1959.
> *Cassell's New Latin Dictionary; Latin-English, English-Latin.* 1960.
> *Cassell's Spanish Dictionary; Spanish-English, English-Spanish.* 1960.
> *The New Cassell's French Dictionary; French-English, English-French.* 1962.
> *The New Cassell's German Dictionary; German-English, English-German.* c1962.
> *Langenscheidt's New Muret-Sanders Encyclopedic Dictionary of the English and German Languages.* 1962–1963. 2 vols.
> *Larousse Modern French-English Dictionary.* c1960.
> *New Complete Russian-English Dictionary.* 1959.

ENCYCLOPEDIAS

The encyclopedia, like the dictionary, has been used at home or at school by nearly everyone. Most encyclopedias are in a number of volumes and are alphabetically arranged—a term that needs explanation. Some of them are arranged alphabetically by *large subject;* others, by minutely alphabetized small subject. For instance, the *Encyclopaedia Britannica* treats "Anglo-Saxon Literature" as a subtopic under "English Literature" (Earliest Times to Chaucer), while the *Encyclopedia Americana* treats it in a separate article, "Anglo-Saxon Literature," in an entirely different volume from "English Literature." The former type, to be of greatest use, needs an index volume to disclose the location of small subjects.

Before using any encyclopedia, check to see if it is arranged *word by word* or *letter by letter* (see pp. 21–22).

Some encyclopedias are kept up to date by the publication of revised editions at intervals of several years. If the interval between editions is long, an occasional supplementary volume is published. Others are kept up to date by yearbooks.

Encyclopaedia Britannica. c1965. 24 vols. Has been considered the most "distinguished" encyclopedia in English, particularly fine in "cultural" fields. The alphabetical arrangement is *letter by letter;* since the information is grouped under large subjects, the index volume is essential for locating small subjects or subdivisions of a large one.

Its long articles are signed with initials, identifiable from the list of contributors in the front; good bibliographies and illustrations. Pronunciation not usually given. The last or 14th edition is more popular in style and treatment than the very scholarly and fine 11th edition and now provides continuous revision in the yearly reprints. Also, the index volume has an atlas and atlas index. The *Britannica Book of the Year*, first published in 1938, is an excellent annual supplement.

Encyclopedia Americana. c1965. 30 vols. An excellent general encyclopedia with emphasis on North America. Alphabetical by *words;* index volume, which is necessary for locating small subjects not covered by cross references; many articles signed; bibliographies. Pronunciation is given. Yearly printings provide continual revision, and it is kept up to date by the *Americana Annual* (a yearbook).

It formerly gave more attention to applied sciences, technology, business, and government; but recent revisions give more adequate treatment to the arts, humanities, and the social sciences. Some articles are accompanied by lists of technical terms with their definitions (glossaries). A useful feature is the history and development of each century under the name of the century, that is, *Fifteenth Century, Eighteenth Century* with a chronological list of events of the century. Preceding the general index in the last volume is an illustrated chronology of world events of the past five years, alphabetical by subject, then chronological under each subject.

Collier's Encyclopedia. 1966. 24 vols. A general encyclopedia with excellent illustrations and many cross references. The articles are signed with full names. Alphabetical *letter* by *letter.* The final volume includes all of the bibliographies and the general index. Kept up to date, in addition to annual printings, by *Collier's Year Book.*

Chambers's Encyclopaedia. 1965. 15 vols. Looseleaf supplement, 1965. Scholarly encyclopedia with British viewpoint and particularly good scientific articles. Contains excellent bibliographies, illustrations, and text. Alphabetical *letter by letter,* many articles signed with initials. An atlas, atlas index and gazetteer, a classified list of subjects, and the subject index are in the last volume.

Encyclopedia International. 1963. 20 vols. Completely new

encyclopedia in its first edition, for students and adults, it has primarily short or "specific-entry" articles, many signed with full names. Numerous cross references, especially good for the nonspecialist. Alphabetical *letter* by *letter*, few bibliographies. Extensive subject index in the last volume.

Compton's Pictured Encyclopedia. c1966. The clear, simple articles in this profusely illustrated encyclopedia serve admirably as a background for more advanced reference books.

The up-to-dateness of this encyclopedia is assured by continuous revision, and by *Compton Yearbook,* equally applicable to text and to illustration. A special feature is the Fact Index, which lists entries indexing the encyclopedia text and short items of information not included in the text in a single alphabetical arrangement in the back of each volume.

The World Book Encyclopedia. 1966. 20 vols. This is another encyclopedia on the level of *Compton's.* Alphabetical word by word, it gives pronunciation, has good cross references, profuse illustrations, and articles signed with full names. The clear, uninvolved presentation is executed in a most attractive format and is not only continuously revised but is also kept up to date by *The World Book Year Book.*

Columbia Encyclopedia. 1963. 3rd ed. A one-volume encyclopedia, very useful when exhaustive articles are not needed. Brief bibliographies, a few illustrations. Gives pronunciation.

Many excellent encyclopedias in special fields—the sciences and technology, religion, the social sciences, education, history, and many others—should be used for fuller information on subjects within their scope than is given in the general encyclopedias listed above. There are many useful foreign-language encyclopedias. Some are:

Enciclopedia Italiana di Scienze, Lettere ed Arti. 1929–1939. 36 vols. *Appendice I, II, III,* 1938–1949. 3 vols. *Appendice 1949–1960.* 2 vols.

Enciclopedia Universal Ilustrada Europeo-Americana. 1907?–1930. 70 vols. in 72. *Appendice, 1930–1933.* 10 vols. *Suplemento Anual, 1934–1960.* 1935–

Grand Larousse Encyclopédique. c1960–1964. 10 vols.

La Grande Encyclopedie. 1885–1901?. 32 vols.

Larousse du XXe Siecle. 1928–1933. 6 vols.
  Supplement. c1953.

Der Grosse Brockhaus. 1952–1957. 12 vols. *Ergänzungsband.*
  c1958. *Sweiter Ergänzungsband, A-Z.* 1963. 1 vol.

YEARBOOKS
AND
HANDBOOKS

Among the most useful books in the library are the yearbooks. They are interesting, too, because they contain facts and figures on subjects within the range of our own experience. We have all read the headlines, at least, during the past year.

Certain yearbooks that are general in scope, planned to bring up to date the information covered by general encyclopedias, are published as the annual supplements to those encyclopedias. Other yearbooks are rather general in scope but are not supplements to encyclopedias and are not necessarily limited to the developments of a single year. Still others deal with a special field of interest or a particular country. The United States government publishes many valuable yearbooks.

Yearbooks are valuable for historical research because they are prepared and published shortly after events occur; they are contemporary with events and reflect contemporary opinion. Almost all of the yearbooks cover events of the *previous year*. For instance, the *Americana Annual* 1966 has as its subtitle *An Encyclopedia of the Events of* 1965; the *Britannica Book of the Year* 1966 has the subtitle *A Record of the March of Events of* 1965. Both of these were published in 1966; therefore, they could not cover 1966. Regardless of the date given as part of the title of a yearbook, consult the publication date on the title page or the copyright date on the back of the title page to be sure of the *date* of the material in the book.

A *handbook* is usually thought of as dealing with the subject matter of a profession, skill, or technique; but those discussed in this chapter more nearly resemble yearbooks in a special field.

ENCYCLOPEDIA SUPPLEMENTS

Americana Annual. 1923–date. This is the yearly supplement to the *Encyclopedia Americana,* with the same world-wide, general coverage. Excellent record of events of the year previous to publication. Alphabetical by *words,* well illustrated, major articles signed, cross references. Index cumulates every few years to reveal the contents of previous volumes. In the front is a "Chronology of the Year" in two parts: date chronology of the year and a topical survey of the year. In the front is a calendar of news events, and in the back is a list of books of the year, classified by subject.

Britannica Book of the Year. 1938–date. Began publication in 1938 to keep the *Encyclopaedia Britannica* always current, and covers the previous year. It has the scope of its encyclopedia, but its presentation is in the dramatic manner of our time, the illustrations typifying the year rather than the editors' viewpoint. Articles are signed with initials; the index is cumulative and is indispensable in locating information not appearing in the *letter-by-letter* alphabetical arrangement. Several feature articles on important topics of the year are in the front; also, a calendar of notable events of the year.

Important material from the yearbooks for 1937–1946 has been assembled into a four-volume work, *10 Eventful Years.*

New International Yearbook. 1908–date. Originally published as the annual supplement to the *New International Encyclopaedia* (now out of print). General in scope, factual in style, alphabetical *letter by letter,* very few cross references or illustrations, noncumulative index. Rather brief information, but major articles are signed.

Collier's Encyclopedia Year Book. 1939–date. Annual supplement to *Collier's Encyclopedia* and a review of national and international events for the previous year. Alphabetical *letter by letter,* signed articles, good illustrations, many *see* references, and a very detailed cumulative index.

Compton Yearbook. 1958–date. A summary and interpretation of the year's events to supplement *Compton's Pictured Encyclopedia.* It offers a chronology of the previous year and a calendar of the current year. Good for quick reference and interesting reading.

World Book Year Book. 1962–date. This is an annual supplement to the World Book Encyclopedia. Arranged in five sections: (1) The Year in Focus, (2) Year Book Special Reports, (3) Main yearbook—the Year on File, (4) *World Book* supplement, (5) Dictionary supplement. These sections are followed by a general index. The main articles are signed, no bibliographies, good illustrations, cross references.

GENERAL

World Almanac, 1868–date, *Information Please Almanac,* 1947–date, and *Reader's Digest Almanac,* 1966–date contain more miscellaneous information than any other reference books. They give recent facts and figures over a wide range of subjects, international in scope, as well as much out-of-the-way data. The *Information Please Almanac* has more general articles (signed) than the other two, and its treatment of foreign countries is fuller and more readable. Two of its useful features are the "Headline Stories of 1965" and "News Chronology of 1965." A section of "Space Age News Chronology" is given in the 1966 volume. *Reader's Digest Almanac* has "World in Review." These features are repeated with current information each year.

None of the three almanacs is alphabetical, but all have good indexes—*World Almanac* index is in front.

A decided advantage of these yearbooks is their "up-to-dateness" because of prompt publication; and they supplement each other.

Annual Register of World Events. 1758–date. A good review of the year, wide in scope. Not alphabetical; full table of contents and a detailed index. Subtitle variations during the years.

Yearbook of World Affairs. 1947–date. English publication arranged by chapters signed by the authors. Table of contents also lists authors of articles. Each chapter has a bibliography at the beginning. Index in back.

The Lincoln Library of Essential Information. 1961. A wealth of information arranged in twelve sections, with full table of contents and detailed subject index. Many cross references and a bibliography at the end of each section.

Famous First Facts; A Record of First Happenings, Discoveries and Inventions in the United States. 1964. Interesting and useful reference book. Arranged by subject with four indexes—by years; by days of the month; to personal names; geographical. Many cross references.

Another helpful book is *Guinness Book of World Records,* c1964.

GEOGRAPHICAL

Yearbooks are published for almost every country, giving the most important facts and figures for the country. It is impossible to list more than a few here, primarily for multiple countries and a few for individual countries noted at the end of the chapter; but many others are available in your library.

American Yearbook. 1910–1950. This yearbook has discontinued publication but is eminently useful for the years covered. Good narrative accounts of events and progress during the year in the United States and her territories at that time, and articles on international affairs affecting the United States. Arranged by large subject, with detailed index and table of contents.

Book of the States. 1935–date. Annual volume with two supplements, giving information for each state in the United States on government and on legislative and administrative personnel.

Canadian Almanac and Directory. 1848–date. Contains information on the government of each province, educational institutions, banking, federal government, legal directory, associations and societies, religious organizations, etc. Not alphabetical, full index in back.

Canada Yearbook, 1905–date, is another useful volume.

Europa Year Book. 1959–date. Supersedes *Europa; The Encyclopedia of Europe.* 1930–1958. A new publication growing out of the trends toward European unity. Pt. 1—European organizations such as NATO, Organization for European Economic Cooperation, Western European Union, United Nations in Europe, The European Community (including the Common Market), and so forth. Pt. 2—European countries, alphabetically arranged, giving a statistical survey, the constitution, government, political parties, finance, trade and industry, world of learning, and so forth. Full table of contents but no index. Comprehensive and well-organized.

International Year Book and Statesmen's Who's Who. 1953–date. Excellent annual, published in Britain. Pt. 1—Fine articles on timely subjects, varying with each annual. Also, International Organizations, Reigning Royal Families of the World, Foreign Ministries of the world in charts, maps. Pt. 2—States of the world and pertinent information for each. Pt. 3—Thousands of brief biographies of contemporary statesmen of the world.

Statesman's Year-Book. 1864–date. Statistical and historical annual of the world. Being a British publication, it treats international organizations, the British Commonwealth and Empire, the United States, and then the other nations of the world. Full index in the back.

South American Handbook. 1924–date. A useful guide to the countries and resources of South and Central America, Mexico, and Cuba, with a good general index in the front.

GOVERNMENT PUBLICATIONS

United States Government Organization Manual. 1934–date. Includes the Constitution of the United States, information on all branches of government, with personnel, official duties, and authority. Very useful. Not alphabetical but has an index of personal names and a detailed subject index.

Congressonal Directory. 1809–date. Useful information about the United States government and about Congress and its members, biographical data on the Cabinet members, diplomatic and consular services, and so forth. Publication during each session of Congress keeps committee appointments and other information up to date. Individual names index in the back; table of contents for *subjects* in the front.

Statistical Abstract of the United States. 1878–date. Standard summary of statistics on the social, political, and economic organization of the United States. Introductory text to each section, source notes below each table of statistics. Annotated table of contents, detailed index. Condensed supplements to the annual abstract are *Historical Statistics of the United States, 1610–1957,* 1960.

Congressional Quarterly Almanac. 1945–date. Readable and popular in treatment, no political bias. Composed of the *Weekly Report* (bills introduced and enacted, committee roundup, floor action, vote charts, week in Congress, Presidential report, and so forth; to this report is published a quarterly cross-reference cumulative index, providing a quick means of relating past events to new action as it occurs) and the *Almanac,* which organizes the past year's material by subject matter instead of chronologically, for permanent reference. Explains how a bill is passed.

This is not published by the United States Government, but it is indispensable for government publications.

Yearbook of Agriculture. 1894–date. Each yearly volume treats a different phase of agriculture in the United States—Climate and Man, Insects, Marketing, Land. The 1965 yearbook is called *Consumers All.* Excellent and readable, illustrated. Fully annotated table of contents, detailed index.

UNITED NATIONS PUBLICATIONS

Statistical Year Book. 1948–date. Annual publication of the United Nations Secretariat, Statistical Office. Gives statistics for agriculture and industrial production, population, manpower, manufacturing, transport, public finance, education and culture, communications, and social conditions. The table of contents, introduction, and indexes (subject index, country index) are given in English and in French. Supplemented by a monthly bulletin.

Yearbook of the United Nations. 1946/47–date. Readable coverage of the activities of the United Nations, illustrated with many charts and tables. Pt. 1—The United Nations, political and security questions, economic and social questions, trusteeship system. Pt. 2—Intergovernmental organizations related to the United Nations. Appendixes and a detailed index.

Useful information can be obtained also from the *Yearbook of Labour Statistics,* 1935/36–date, and from the *Demographic Yearbook,* 1948–date. The latter deals with a study of populations.

OTHER YEARBOOKS AND HANDBOOKS

Some other useful yearbooks and handbooks are:

SCIENCE AND TECHNOLOGY

McGraw-Hill Yearbook of Science and Technology. 1962–date. Keeps up to date the *Encyclopedia of Science and Technology* with a comprehensive coverage of the important events of the previous year. It has numerous feature articles, a special pictorial section featuring outstanding scientific photographs of the past year. Then comes the alphabetical arrangement with signed articles, bibliographies, cross references, and illustrations. A list of contributors and the index are in the back.

Handbook of Chemistry and Physics; A Ready Reference Book of Chemical and Physical Data. 1913–date. Contains a large amount of accurate, reliable and up-to-date information in condensed form for the two physical sciences of chemistry and physics and closely allied sciences. Extensive index in back. *The Handbook of Mathematical Tables,* c1964, is a supplement to the above.

Chemical Engineers' Handbook. c1963. Based on unit-operation concept as practical approach to the application of chemical engineers and students. Arranged by subject sections with a full index in the back giving section and page references. Voluminous illustrations.

Mathematical Handbook for Scientists and Engineers; Definitions, Theorems and Formulas for Reference and Review. 1961. This is for both the undergraduate and the graduate level. It concludes with numerical tables and a glossary of symbols and notations. Arranged by chapters with a bibliography at the end of each. Annotated table of contents and a full index.

Handbook of Geophysics. 1960. Provides text, tables, and

charts dealing with the atmosphere, wind, temperature, precipitation, clouds, geomagnetism, meteors, the ionosphere, thermal radiation, the sun, cosmic radiation, atmospheric exploratory devices, and other subjects. It is arranged by chapters with a bibliography at the end of each. Signed articles, illustrations. Index in back. The first edition was called *Handbook of Geophysics for Air Force Designers.*

Aerospace Yearbook. 1919–1961. From 1919 through 1959 this was entitled *Aircraft Yearbook.* Publication temporarily suspended after 1961. It covers areospace events, the industry, military aviation, civil aviation, research and development, government and aviation, production, missiles. Arranged by topics, with an index. In the back is a day-by-day chronology for the previous year.

Agricultural Engineers' Handbook. 1961. Covers crop-production equipment, soil and water conservation, farmstead structures and equipment, basic agricultural data. Arranged by sections with chapters under each, signed by specialists. Illustrated, includes a bibliography and a full index. Another useful volume is *Agricultural Engineers Yearbook,* 1945–date.

SOCIAL SCIENCE

Encyclopedia of Social Work. 1929–date. Publication a bit irregular. Was, until 1960, the *Social Work Year Book.* The scope is now broadened and it is an authoritative source of information on social work and social welfare, mostly restricted to the United States and Canada. Longer articles are signed. Bibliographies; full index in the back.

World Year Book of Education. 1931–date. Formerly was *Yearbook of Education,* until 1965. Covers "The Education Explosion" world-wide. Arranged by chapters, with a full table of contents and a brief index.

Commodity Year Book. 1942–date. Information on current commodity events as they unfold, from commodity exchanges, governmental agencies, trade associations, and other organizations. Alphabetical by commodity, no index.

Economic Almanac. 1940–date. A handbook on business, labor, and government in the United States and other areas, chiefly Canada. Point of view of practical business and the general public interest. Detailed index, followed by Canadian index.

Political Handbook and Atlas of the World. 1927–date. Formerly called *Political Handbook of the World.* Designed to furnish the necessary factual background for understanding political events in all countries that have independent governments; colonies and trust territories not included. Alphabetical by major countries, followed by small or recently independent countries. Table of contents in front but no index.

NATIONAL

Anglo-American Year Book, 1913–date.
British Commonwealth, 1956–date.
India, A Reference Annual, 1953–date.
Japan Annual, 1954–date.
Whitaker's Almanack (British), 1896–date.

SCIENCE

American Institute of Physics Handbook, c1963.
Biochemists' Handbook, c1959.
Civil Engineering Handbook, c1963.
Handbook of Microbiology, c1960.
Industrial Engineering Handbook, c1963.
Manual of Field Geology, c1962.
Nuclear Engineering Handbook, 1958.
Nuclear Handbook, 1958.

AUTOMATION

Computer Handbook, 1962.
Data Processing Yearbook, 1959–date.
Handbook for Automation, Computation and Control,
    1958–1961. 3 vols.

HUMANITIES

International Television Almanac, 1955–date.
International Motion Picture Almanac, 1929–date.
Handbook of Greek Mythology, 1958.
The New Century Classical Handbook, c1962.
Poetry Handbook, 1962.
Writers' and Artists' Year Book, 1907–date.
Yearbook of Comparative and General Literature, 1952–date.

LABOR

International Labor Directory and Handbook, 1950–date.

SCIENCE
AND
TECHNOLOGY

Development in all fields of science and technology has progressed so phenomenally in the last few years that it is imperative to add a number of reference books covering these areas of investigation and achievement in preparing this edition. It must be recognized that progress is so rapid that information is quickly out of date; therefore, some of the books in this chapter may be slightly out of date by the time this book goes to press.

Any reputable researcher should make it a consistent policy to check the usual sources for the *latest editions* of published reference books and for new ones published in his field of specialization. Certainly such a policy is especially important in science and technology.

Most professions produce handbooks of their trade (see p. 64). There are excellent ones in all scientific and technical professions. Only a few such handbooks are included in this chapter. The card catalog in any library will reveal those not listed here. The same is true of dictionaries, glossaries, and encyclopedias of a specialized field.

The *most recent* developments in science and technology can easily be located through indexes to the periodical literature in such fields.

History of Technology. 1954–1958. This five-volume reference work provides students of technology and applied science with some humane and historical background and a longer perspective of the ways in which the immensely complex technical knowledge of our civilization has come into being, a history of how things have been done or made.

Excellent set, well illustrated. Chronologically arranged, with numerous indexes in the back of each volume—personal names, place names, subjects. Each chapter is by a specialist whose name is given. Extensive bibliographies and lists of references.

ENCYCLOPEDIAS

McGraw-Hill Encyclopedia of Science and Technology. 2nd ed. c1966. 15 vols. Authoritative, comprehensive coverage of the physical, natural, and applied sciences, international in scope. Biographical and historical aspects excluded. Most useful for college and university undergraduates and to laymen interested in scientific fields. An introductory article generally provides a broad survey of each branch of science, and separate articles cover the main subdivisions and more specific aspects of it.

Most articles are signed with initials (list of contributors in the back), extensive illustrations, many cross references and bibliographies. Vol. 15 is the full index to the set, with a classified topical index in the back. Kept up to date by *McGraw-Hill Yearbook of Science and Technology.*

Encyclopedia of the Sciences. c1963. This work is for students, teachers, and scientists interested in fields other than their own. Illustrations, cross references, no bibliographies, but a full index. "Important Events in Science" in the back.

The Harper Encyclopedia of Science. 1963. 4 vols. Well-rounded, brief explanations, all signed with initials. In the back of vol. 4 is a list of authors, an extensive bibliography classified by subject, and a general index.

Encyclopedia of Chemical Technology. c1963-1969. Will be in approximately 20 volumes, completed in 1969. Being published at the rate of three volumes a year—eight were released through 1965, three more in 1966. Designed to present the entire field of chemical technology for professional chemists and chemical engineers, for those in industry and in university and other research institutions. Should help in training students.

Alphabetical, and the last volume will be the full index. Bibliographies, signed articles, cross references.

Encyclopedia of Chemistry. c1957. *Supplement,* 1958. Broad scope, from the viewpoint of the chemist. Remarkably well-condensed information. Alphabetical and has an index, cross references, and illustrations.

Encyclopedic Dictionary of Physics: General, Nuclear, Solid State, Molecular, Geophysics, Biophysics and Related Subjects. 1961–1964. 9 vols. Long-needed tool, with articles of graduate or near-graduate calibre. More encyclopedic than dictionary. Signed articles, bibliographies, cross references, with a list of contributors in the front of each volume. Vol. 8 is composed of a complete subject index to the other 7 vols. and an author index to those volumes. Vol. 9 is a multilingual glossary.

Van Nostrand's Scientific Encyclopedia. c1958. Basic reference work on science and engineering and on mathematics and medicine, including aeronautics, astronomy, botany, chemistry, electronics and radio, geology, engineering, computer technology, guided missiles, nuclear science and engineering, physics, zoology, etc. *Progressive discussion* of each topic. Valuable to laymen, students, and trained scientists.

Alphabetical, well illustrated, extensive bibliographies.

International Encyclopedia of Chemical Science. 1964. A new encyclopedia of chemical terms for chemists and non-chemists, teachers and students, and those interested in pure or applied chemistry, chemical research, engineering, or technology. Explanations as well as definitions. Four multilingual indexes in the back: French-English, German-English, Russian-English, Spanish-English.

Encyclopedia of Industrial Chemical Analysis. 1966–? 20 vols. Three volumes were published in 1966, and the set will be completed at the rate of three volumes per year. The first three volumes cover general techniques, the index being in the third volume. The remaining volumes will be devoted to the *analysis of specific materials.* At this date, it is undecided whether or not the index to vols. 4-20 will be in the last volume or published periodically in several of the volumes.

Audel's Encyclopedia of Space Science. c1963. 4 vols. Each scientific or technological segment of the 4 volumes contains comprehensive information—space and science travel, the world of the atom, electronics, computers, automation, and many other new sciences.

Alphabetical, abundantly illustrated with photographs, sketches, technical drawings, diagrams, flow charts, schematics, graphs. The index is in the back of vol. 4.

Space Encyclopedia. 1960. A guide to astronomy and space research; brings together basic information on celestial mechanics and the astronomy of the solar system in their unity with electronics and mechanical engineering. Alphabetical and well illustrated, has cross references.

Guide to Space. 1959. Complete compendium of terms of modern space technology and guided missilery. Alphabetical.

The Universal Encyclopedia of Mathematics. 1964. This translation of a German work is a popular reference book, reliable and clear. Alphabetical by subject, it has a collection of formulas in the back. No index.

Engineering Encyclopedia. c1954. Old but very useful. A condensed encyclopedia and mechanical dictionary for engineers, mechanics, technical schools, industrial plants. Essential facts about 4500 engineering subjects. Alphabetical, cross references, no index.

Encyclopedia of the Biological Sciences. 1961. Defines, describes, and explains subjects covered by the broad field of the biological sciences. Alphabetical *word by word*, with signed articles, a list of contributors, illustrations, cross references. Index in the back.

DICTIONARIES

Chambers's Technical Dictionary. 1958. Definitions of terms important in pure and applied sciences, for laymen as well as for scientist. Alphabetical and brief. Supplement in the back for new terms relating to advances in science and technology.

Hackh's Chemical Dictionary. 1967. Comprehensive dictionary of terms generally used in chemistry and many of those used in related sciences. American and British usage given. Alphabetical.

Condensed Chemical Dictionary. c1961. Useful for quick

access to essential data on chemicals and other substances used in manufacturing and research, and to terms in general use in chemistry and the process industries. Alphabetical.

International Dictionary of Physics and Electronics. 1961. Simple definitions and strict discussions of terms of pure science and its applications. International in scope. For professional physicists, students, and workers in the field. Alphabetical, cross references, illustrated with diagrams and formulas. Multilingual index in the back.

International Dictionary of Applied Mathematics. c1960. Defines the terms and describes the methods in applications of mathematics to 31 fields of physical science and engineering. Illustrated with diagrams, formulas, etc., cross references. Multilingual indexes in the back.

Aeronautical Dictionary. 1964. Prepared by NASA. Comprehensive, authoritative aeronautical dictionary for wide audience—professionals, nonprofessionals, novices. Also, certain fundamental terms in related fields. Alphabetical, cross references, lengthy bibliographies in the back, classified by type of publication.

Dictionary of Technical Terms for Aerospace Use. 1965. Published by NASA. "Attempts to define the meanings of selected terms in use in areas of activity of the National Aeronautics and Space Administration. This is necessary because of rapid language growth, and exactness and precision are lacking with such growth; because such is of grave importance to scientists and engineers." Designed for use by persons with scientific or engineering education who are studying outside their field of specialty, but also made as clear as possible for the nonexpert. Largely technical.

Alphabetical, cross references, brief bibliography of primary sources.

Jane's All the World's Aircraft. 1909—date. Annual publication from Britain. Excellent and useful reference book in the field of aeronautics, well illustrated with all types of aircraft in all countries. Not alphabetical, detailed general index which also refers to previous editions followed by three classified indexes: Rotary wing aircraft, Jet engines, Piston engines.

Blakiston's New Gould Medical Dictionary. 1965. Modern,

comprehensive dictionary of terms used in all branches of medicine and allied sciences, including medical physics and chemistry, dentistry, pharmacy, nursing, veterinary medicine, zoology and botany, in medicolegal terms.

Alphabetical, brief definitions, pronunciations, large section of illustrations with many color plates, cross references. Appendix of useful tables.

Dorland's Illustrated Medical Dictionary. 1957. Alphabetical *letter by letter;* brief definitions; pronunciations; cross references.

Two other useful and recent publications are *Stedman's Medical Dictionary,* 1961, and *Elsevier's Medical Dictionary in Five Languages,* 1964.

Some other useful reference books in Science and Technology:

> *Dictionary of Technical Terms,* c1961. 9th ed. rev.
> *A Dictionary of Science Terms,* 1965.
> *Concise Chemical and Technical Dictionary,* 1962, 2nd enl. ed.
> *Space Age Dictionary,* 1963, 2nd ed.
> *Dictionary of Astronautics,* c1964.
> *Elsevier's Dictionary of Aeronautics in Six Languages,* 1964.
> *Elsevier's Dictionary of Nuclear Science and Technology in Six Languages,* 1958.
> *Encyclopedic Dictionary of Electronics and Nuclear Engineering,* 1959.
> *Elsevier's Dictionary of General Physics in Six Languages,* 1962.
> *Dictionary of Physics,* 1958.
> *Elsevier's Dictionary of Automation, Computers, Control and Measuring in Six Languages,* 1961.
> *The Crescent Dictionary of Mathematics,* 1962.
> *A Dictionary of Geology,* 1961.
> *A Dictionary of Biology,* 1962.

HISTORY
AND THE
SOCIAL
SCIENCES

Only a few refence books on history and the social sciences can be given here. Although many good ones in the field of history are limited as to time or place, the present list, except for books on American history, will be confined to those of general scope.

HISTORY

Worldmark Encyclopedia of the Nations. c1963. 2nd ed. 5 vols. Different from any encyclopedia produced in recent years, reflects the life of men and nations in the age of science, the great turning point in history. Political framework is filled in by a comprehensive survey of major interests of people everywhere, should provide an understanding of our time. Authoritative.

Covers 135 countries: Vol. 1—Asia and Australia; vol. 2—Africa; vol. 3—America; vol. 4—Europe; vol. 5—United Nations. Each volume is alphabetical by country, with full maps on the end papers and small maps with each country. Index only to vol. 5 in the back.

Encyclopedia of World History. 1952. A chronological outline of historical facts covering ancient, medieval, and modern history through 1950. Emphasizes political, military, and diplomatic history. In the back is a list of events from January 1,

1951 to April 30, 1952. Very extensive index in the back; illustrated, cross references. Useful appendixes.

Encyclopedia of American History. c1961. Rev. and enl. ed. Essential historical facts about American life and institutions, dates, events, achievements, and persons. Very readable. Preliminary articles on "Beginnings," but main information begins with 1578 and goes through January 1961.

Pt. 1—Basic chronology of major political and military events; Pt. 2—Topical chronology of nonpolitical aspects of American life; Pt. 3—Biographical section of 400 notable Americans, alphabetically arranged. The very full index is essential to the effective use of the book.

Album of American History. 1944–1949. 5 vols. A pictorial history of the United States, accompanied by brief, excellent text, from the Colonial period to the beginning of World War I. The fifth volume is a superior index.

Pageant of America. 1925–1929. 15 vols. Another pictorial history of the United States from Indian times to 1924. It covers unusual rather than ordinary historical events, with more text than in the *Album of American History.* Each volume deals with a broad subject; its pictures are chronologically arranged. An index in each volume; the final volume, a topical guide.

Dictionary of American History. 1942. 6 vols. A series of brief, compact, signed articles covering American history in its widest sense, principally political, economic, social, industrial, and cultural history. Authoritative. Index volume for additional information on *related* articles.

The Dictionary of American History. 1963. Chiefly for verification and identification; brief information. Alphabetical, many cross references, no index. Chronology of American history in the front.

The Encyclopedia of American Facts and Dates. 1962. Vast number of interesting events. Chronologically arranged from earliest times to the present, with four fields of interest arranged in parallel columns. Very exhaustive index.

10 Eventful Years. 1947. A record of events of the years before, during, and after World War II, covering 1937–1946, and compiled from material in the *Britannica Book of the Year.*

Wide in scope, encyclopedic in form and content, well illustrated, and readable. Excellent bibliographies, many cross references, and a detailed index.

American Book of Days. c1948. Contains information about holidays, festivals, notable anniversaries, and holy days, giving their history and the customs of celebrating them here and in other countries. The second edition lists significant days of World War II and other fairly recently established dates of commemoration. Chronologically arranged, with a full index.

Dictionary of European History. c1954. Concise, reliable information concerning most of the events and prominent personalities from A.D. 500 in European history. Brief articles, alphabetically arranged.

Latin American History; A Summary of Political, Economic, Social and Cultural Events. 1963. 5th ed. A brief summary of facts about the history of Latin America. Full table of contents; good bibliography and full index in the back.

Another useful work is *History of Latin America from the Beginning to the Present,* 1961.

Some other useful reference books in history are: *New Larned History for Ready Reference,* 12 volumes, 1922; *Historical Abstracts,* 1775–1945; *Documents of American History,* c1963, 7th ed.; *Everyman's Dictionary of Dates,* c1964, 4th ed.; *A Chronology and Fact Book of the United Nations, 1941–1964,* 1964, 2nd ed.

SOCIAL SCIENCES

Encyclopaedia of the Social Sciences. 1930–1935. This 15-volume work is the only one covering all of the social sciences. It is international in scope and very readable. Its articles are written and signed by specialists; a large proportion are biographies. Its bibliographies and cross references are excellent. The arrangement is alphabetical; the last volume has a general index. A reprint edition, 1948, has eight volumes (two in one), but the index indicates volume numbers in the 15-volume set.

Much confusion exists in the minds of students as to *what* the social sciences are. The following list, showing the range of subjects covered, should help: political science, economics, law, anthropology (the races of mankind), sociology, social work, social aspects (human relations) of education, psychology, biology, geography, art, and medicine. In other words, social sciences show man in his relation to the world and to his fellow beings.

A Dictionary of the Social Sciences. c1964. Prepared under the auspices of UNESCO. "Designed to describe and define approximately one thousand basic concepts used in the social sciences." Its purpose is to present a general introduction to the main problems and developments in the social sciences to students and to those working in the field, and to inform specialists in other fields. Alphabetical.

Dictionary of Social Science. c1959. Specialized vocabularies in the present era prevent understanding by other groups; therefore, this volume is most useful for definitions of terms used in the social sciences. Useful to the specialist, the student, and the layman. Cross references, no pronunciation given.

Encyclopedia of Educational Research. 1960. 3rd ed. This excellent tool aids students, teachers, and administrators by bringing together studies done in the educational field to 1960 and evaluates and interprets them. Has dated and signed articles and excellent, lengthy bibliographies. The index is in the *middle* of the book on colored pages.

Dictionary of Education. 1959. Comprehensive dictionary of professional terms in education. Alphabetical, with cross references. In the back are alphabetical lists of terms and definitions for education in Canada, England, France, Germany, and Italy.

Dictionary of Political Science. c1964. Concise definitions and descriptions of terms, events, and personalities most frequently encountered in the literature of political science. For teachers, students, and laymen. Full introduction, every definition signed with the author's initials (list of contributors in front), cross references. Short appendix in the back with cross references from the main work.

The American Political Dictionary. c1962. Technical language of political science and American government, provides basic comprehension of institutions, practices and problems involving 1100 terms, agencies, court cases, and statutes. Arranged by chapters, each with alphabetically arranged sections. Full index.

Three other useful volumes are *American Political Terms;*

An Historical Dictionary, 1962, giving historical facts as background for each word; *The Crescent Dictionary of American Politics,* 1962; and *An Encyclopedia of Modern World Politics,* 1950.

The New Business Encyclopedia. c1963. Many will be helped by this reference tool. Full table of contents, detailed index with cross references. Illustrated with tables and charts. Another one is *2001 Business Terms and What They Mean,* c1962.

Glenn G. Munn's Encyclopedia of Banking and Finance. c1962. 6th ed. rev. Comprehensive, accurate, convenient explanation of the financial system. Cross references; bibliographies at the ends of articles or definitions. Alphabetical. A dictionary in the field is *Encyclopedic Dictionary of Business Finance,* c1960.

Geography

Columbia Lippincott Gazetteer of the World with 1961 Supplement. c1962. A gazetteer is a geographical dictionary. This one covers every type of geographical location and feature in the world, giving pronunciation of each, as well as important information. The 1960 Census and new nations and geographical changes are in the supplement.

Much geographical information is found also in atlases, in the *World Almanac,* and in Ayer's *Directory of Newspapers and Periodicals,* which is published annually and covers Canada, the United States, and the West Indies, with maps. The *Columbia Encyclopedia* and the *Century Cyclopedia of Names* are useful for the identification of geographical names.

Webster's Geographical Dictionary. c1962. Lists names from earliest times to the immediate past, giving information and pronunciation, with numerous maps. For the United States the 1960 Census is used; but for Canada and the United Kingdom, the 1951 one is used.

Shepherd's Historical Atlas. 1956. The best of the small, general historical atlases, covering the period 1450 B.C.–A.D. 1929, with a supplement of historical maps since 1929. The full index in the back indicates an entry that is a geographical feature other than a town or city. Read the statement at the beginning of the index to understand exactly how to use the atlas. *Atlas of World History*, 1957, and *European History Atlas* . . . , c1951, are useful.

Atlas of American History. 1943. Contains the geographical history of the United States, arranged by date from the voyages of discovery to 1912. Supplements the *Dictionary of American History.* Another useful one is the *Historical Atlas of the United States*, 1953.

National Geographic Atlas of the 50 States. c1960. Fine, detailed maps of the 50 United States and of our National Parks. Extensive index in the back, listing all types of geographical locations.

Prentice-Hall's World Atlas. 1963. Beautifully executed maps, with an index.

Cosmopolitan World Atlas. c1962. All geographical names appear in *one* alphabetical index. Important features of the atlas are: A gazetteer of historical names not usually on maps, a glossary of English equivalents of foreign geographical terms, and an explanation of geographical terms found on the maps. Many supplementary tables. Major periods of world history depicted on maps in a new section.

Rand McNally Commercial Atlas and Marketing Guide. c1966. In two parts: United States; Canada and the rest of the world. A full index follows each United States map, together with many tables of statistics. 1965 population *estimates* are used. Retail sales map of each state. At the beginning of the section on Canada and the rest of the world is a gazetteer index; at the end is a general index of foreign cities and physical features. The atlas provides many supplementary tables that are advantageous.

Hammond's Ambassador World Atlas, 1961, is another helpful one.

Encyclopaedia Britannica World Atlas. c1964. "The World as a Globe" shows projections of areas of the world on a *curved surface*. Includes physical and political maps, geographical comparisons, a glossary of geographical terms, a gazetteer index, geographical summaries and world spheres of influence. Excellent selection of statistical data and bibliographies.

Goode's World Atlas, c1964. This atlas contains physical,

political, and economic maps. Excellent reference tool, with information about map reading and a pronouncing index of geographical names.

National Geographic Atlas of the World. 1963. Detailed, exceedingly fine maps treating the world by geographic regions. A most useful feature is the descriptive text at the beginning of each section. Fine statistical digests follow the country summaries. Global projections with superior accuracy. Chart of temperature and rainfall in 198 cities of the world. Exhaustive index in the back. Very important to read the introduction to the atlas.

Life Pictorial Atlas of the World. 1961. New type of atlas. In front are color maps depicting The Solar System, The Changing Earth, Land Forms of the Earth, Origins of the Weather, Climate Zones, Ocean Currents, etc. Excellent color pictures and descriptive text; uses terrain maps and political maps. One purpose is its use as a guide to understanding man's world in the space age. *One* general index.

Times Atlas of the World. 1955–1960. Published by the London *Times,* in five volumes. More extensive than any other atlas, good maps. Vol. 1—The World, Australia, and East Asia (1958); Vol. 2—India, the Middle East, and Russia (1960); Vol. 3—Northern Europe (1955); Vol. 4—The Mediterranean and Africa (1956); Vol. 5—The Americas (1957).

BIOGRAPHICAL DICTIONARIES

The life stories of famous people are usually interesting, and the books that record them are among the most frequently used in the library. Hardly a course in college does not require their use at some time. With few exceptions, these books have some kind of limitation. Some are limited to living persons; others, to those who have died. Nationality limitation is common to many of them. Still others include only the outstanding people of one profession, as *Who's Who in Aviation, American Men of Science, Who's Who in Electronics,* and *Who's Who in the United Nations.*

Three most important questions that you should ask yourself before looking up a biographical account are: Is the person living or dead? What is his nationality? What is his profession? This procedure will save much time.

UNIVERSAL

New Century Cyclopedia of Names. c1954. This three-volume set consists solely of information about proper names having importance in the English-speaking world, giving precise and detailed facts. Persons, including mythological and legendary persons, places, literary characters, historical events, and so forth. Alphabetical; pronunciation marked for difficult names.

Chambers's Biographical Dictionary. c1962. The great of

all nations and all times, based on articles in *Chambers's Encyclopaedia,* with hundreds of short articles added. Supplement in the front. Pronunciation of difficult or non-English names. Alphabetical.

Dictionary of Universal Biography of All Ages and All Peoples. 1951. Primarily for *identification;* a guide to biographies of prominent men and women, not still living, from earliest history until 1951. Alphabetical.

Universal Pronouncing Dictionary of Biography and Mythology. (1930). Includes brief accounts of famous actual persons in all countries and ages, and of mythical characters. Pronunciations of unusual names are offered, but no illustrations.

Webster's Biographical Dictionary. c1962. Concise biographies of noteworthy persons of all time. Pronunciations are given detailed attention.

Current Biography; Who's News and Why. 1940–date. Universal in scope, giving a biographical sketch of each person, followed by a short bibliography. Numerous pictures. Alphabetical; published *monthly,* with an annual cumulation in December (*Current Biography Yearbook*). The index cumulates back to 1940. The annual volume has a classification by profession and a necrology for the year. Accurate and useful.

International Who's Who. 1935–date. A listing of the world's eminent living personalities. Brief, up-to-date sketches are included, alphabetically arranged. The roster of reigning royal families is an interesting feature. Published annually.

World Biography. 1940–   . From 1940 to 1946 this was *Biographical Encyclopedia of the World.* Published at intervals, the 5th ed. in 1954. Affords world-wide coverage; however, references to the United States, Britain, and Western Europe predominate. A monthly service keeps it up to date. Alphabetical.

ENGLISH

Dictionary of National Biography. 1885–1901. The best reference work for biographies of famous Englishmen (Great Britain and her possessions) who are no longer living. Excellent bibliographies, alphabetical arrangement, but no illustrations.

When the complete set (21 volumes) was published, its excellence required its being kept up to date; so supplements were published from time to time through 1949, and will continue to be published. If the person whose life you are searching for is not included in the main set, be sure to consult the supplements.

The Dictionary of National Biography; The Concise Dictionary Being an Epitome of the Main Work and Its Supplement, c1962, is a two-volume work summarizing the vast contents of the main work. Vol. 1—to 1900; Vol. 2— 1901–1950. At the end of each concise biography there is a reference to volume and page in the main set.

Who's Who. 1849–date. An annual publication about famous living men and women, chiefly English. It gives brief and accurate biographical accounts, including present addresses. Alphabetical, with no pictures.

Who Was Who; A Companion to Who's Who Containing Biographies of Those Who Died during the Period. 1920– Published about every ten years.

AMERICAN

Dictionary of American Biography. 1928–1944. For famous Americans no longer living. Decidedly the best in this field, it is on the same plan as its British counterpart—excellent bibliographies, no illustrations, alphabetical arrangement, and supplements. The index volume is an analysis of the other 20 volumes, giving among its six sections an index of all important *topics* discussed in the set. Another valuable section groups persons according to occupation. Volume 21 (1944) is the first supplement; others will follow.

Concise Dictionary of American Biography, c1964, is an abridgement of the above and is useful for brief, authoritative information.

White's Conspectus of American Biography. 1937. One of the most useful classified lists of Americans who have achieved distinction. It includes, among others, lists of Americans in fiction, poetry, and the drama; pseudonyms and sobriquets; leaders in state and national government, in education, in the arts and sciences, and in the professional fields from Colonial times up to 1937. The anniversary calendar is a useful feature. *White's Conspectus* is a volume in the *National Cyclopedia of American Biography.*

Who's Who in America. 1899–date. On the same plan as *Who's Who,* but limited to Americans and published every two years. Occasionally cross references are made to previous volumes. This means that the persons are still living but have no further noteworthy accomplishments that would necessitate reprinting. A geographical index is in the front. Kept up to date by quarterly supplements. Indexes and necrology will accompany the 60th anniversary edition.

Who Was Who in America, 1942–   , is a companion to the above.

AUTHORS

Twentieth Century Authors. 1942. First supplement, 1955. These two supersede *Living Authors* and *Authors Today and Yesterday.* Offer information on prominent authors of this century in all countries, the accounts being more colorful and entertaining than those in the scholarly or the drab factual books. Alphabetical, and includes a picture of most authors; pronunciation given in the index. *American Authors, 1600–1900,* 1938, done in the same manner, is limited to American authors no longer living.

Masterplots Cyclopedia of World Authors. 1958. 2 vols. International in scope, with good biographical sketches. List of author's works at beginning of article and a bibliography at the end of each. Alphabetical, cross references, and an index of names in the back.

Contemporary Authors. 1962–date. International guide to *current* authors and their works, those being published and read today, including new and relatively unknown authors. Concise but detailed information. Complete bibliographies of authors' works. At intervals a cumulative index covering previous volumes appears in the back of a volume. In vols. 13-14 (1965) there is a list of pseudonyms used by authors in those volumes.

Everyman's Dictionary of Literary Biography, English and American. c1958. (Supersedes *Biographical Dictionary of English Biography.*) Authors of *popular* works, omitting scientists and other scholars. Alphabetical under authors' real names, not pseudonyms. Fuller than *Who's Who*. Has cross references.

British Authors before 1800, c1952, and *British Authors of the Nineteenth Century*, 1936, are two more useful books.

Catholic Authors. 1948. Second volume, 1952. Lists contemporary Catholic authors, living and dead. Foreign authors are included if at least one of their works has been translated into English. Alphabetical, illustrated, with an index in the front.

SCIENTISTS

Asimov's Biographical Encyclopedia of Science and Technology . . . . c1964. "Living stories of more than 1000 great scientists from the Age of Greece to the Space Age." Narrative style of presentation, pronunciation of unusual names. Illustrated. Chronological arrangement with a full index.

American Men of Science. 1965–   . 11th ed. This set covers distinguished men and women now engaged in scientific research. *Who's Who* type of information. Being published in two sections: (1) The Physical and Biological Sciences, (2) The Social and Behavioral Sciences.

The first section, in 6 vols., will be completed late in 1967. The second section will follow after the completion of these volumes. Each section alphabetical.

There will be four supplements to the first section, published semiannually, thus updating the set.

Space Scientists and Engineers: Selected Biographical and Bibliographical Listing, 1957–1961. 1962. Includes scientists who are making significant contributions to the advancement of space science. Brief biographical accounts and bibliographies. Arranged by country, United States first, then alphabetical by other countries. Author index and a subject index.

Leaders in American Science. 1953/54–   . Published every two years. Covers the United States and Canada, typical *Who's Who* type of information, with brief biographies and photographs. Alphabetical.

SCHOLARS IN THE HUMANITIES

Directory of American Scholars. 1942–   . 4th ed. in 4 vols. published in 1963. Includes those scholars working in the fields of philosophy, history, literature, languages, and other related disciplines. Alphabetical, with a list of "received-too-late" in the back.

—Vol. 1—History; vol. 2—English, Speech and Drama;
—vol. 3—Foreign Languages, Linguistics, and Philology;
—vol. 4—Philosophy, Religion, and Law.

There is a *Who's Who* for almost every profession of importance and for many countries in the world, far too many to list here, except for a few examples. Be sure to inquire for such books when needed.

> *Chemical Who's Who*, 1928–date.
> *Who's Who in Engineering*, 1922/23–date.
> *American Architects Directory*, 1962.
> *Who's Who in American Education*, 1928–date.
> *The Biographical Encyclopaedia and Who's Who of the American Theatre*, 1966.
> *Who's Who in American Art*, 1936/37–
> *The Canadian Who's Who*, 1910–date.
> *Who's Who in Latin America* . . . , 1935–   , irregular.
> *Who's Who in the United Nations*, 1951–date.

HUMANITIES: LITERATURE, FINE ARTS, RELIGION

Literature

Reference books in the field of literature are so numerous that it is difficult to make a selection. The Reference or Humanities Librarian will assist you in using those not included here.

WORLD LITERATURE

Cassell's Encyclopedia of World Literature. c1954. Originally, *Cassell's Encyclopedia of Literature,* 1953, published in England. A two-volume set, divided into three parts: Pt. 1—Histories of the literatures of the world; Pt. 2—Biographies of writers who died before August 1, 1941; Pt. 3—Biographies of writers who were living at the outbreak of World War I or who were born after that. Many Asian and Central European authors included. Alphabetical; no index.

Masterpieces of World Literature in Digest Form. Series 3. 1960. All three volumes in this comprehensive collection of plot-stories from world literature are most useful. In this third series the reviews are in *essay* form and not signed. Alphabetical by *title,* with an author index.

Shipley's *Encyclopedia of Literature.* c1946. Two-volume collection of surveys of literature of the world. Alphabetical by national literature, signed articles, bibliographies, and cross references.

Benét's *Reader's Encyclopedia.* c1965. An encyclopedia of world literature and the arts, with articles on topics that the average reader might wish to understand in the course of his reading. It covers characters in literature, authors, individual works, technical terms in literature, epithets and phrases, brief summaries of plays and novels, and so forth. A supplement in the back for more recent material. Alphabetical, wide in scope, useful.

Masterplots. c1964. 6 vols. Essay-reviews, not signed. Vol. 1—Drama Series; vol. 2—American Fiction; vol. 3—English Fiction; vol. 4—European Fiction; vol. 5—Poetry Series; vol. 6—Nonfiction Series. Each volume is arranged by title, with an author index in the back.

Shipley's *Dictionary of World Literature.* 1953. Deals only with literary criticism, literary schools, movements, forms, and terms of the major languages of ancient and modern times. Alphabetical, brief articles (some signed with initials), cross references.

The Concise Encyclopedia of Modern World Literature. c1963. Discussions and criticisms of authors' works, not biographical. At the beginning is a section on "National Literature" and one on "Forms of Literature." The contributors concentrated on writers in English and primarily on the twentieth century. The encyclopedia should "increase the pleasurable scope of good reading."

Alphabetical by author treated, with an author index and a title index. Cross references. Full page pictures of many authors.

Thesaurus of Book Digests; Digests of the World's Permanent Writings from the Ancient Classics to Current Literature. c1949.

Oxford Companion to Classical Literature. c1959. Covers classical allusions in modern literature, dealing with the evolution of classical literature, principal authors and their chief works. Depicts historical, political, social and religious backgrounds, and explains the elements of classical literature—epic, tragedy, comedy, metre, etc. It gives accounts of principal authors and describes the subjects or contents of their works, under author and title.

Arranged by author, title, and subject all in one alphabet and gives pronunciation.

ENGLISH AND EUROPEAN LITERATURE

Cambridge History of English Literature. 1907–1927. The most important history of English literature, in 15 volumes, arranged by periods from earliest times through the nineteenth century. Excellent bibliographies and an index are in the back of each volume. The general index is for the English edition; it is useful only to indicate volumes in the American edition. This indication is sufficient, however, since page references can be located easily through the index in the designated volume.

Baugh's *Literary History of England.* c1948. One-volume history of the literature of England, from earliest times through 1939. Chronologically arranged, with a very full index.

New Century Handbook of English Literature. 1956. Useful reference tool for identifying English writers, works of literature, characters in literature, and various related items. Includes, also, great Irish writers, and those classified as Anglo-American, Canadian, Australian, and South African. Alphabetical, pronunciation given, cross references.

Oxford Companion to English Literature. 1946. A reader's handbook for English literature, doing for one literature what Benét does for world literature. Alphabetical.

Columbia Dictionary of Modern European Literature. 1947. Broad in scope, covering the literatures of continental Europe in the twentieth century and the immediately preceding decades. Biographical sketches of the writers, alphabetical articles signed with initials, and short, chronological bibliographies are included.

AMERICAN LITERATURE

Cambridge History of American Literature. 1917–1921. This four-volume work does for American literature what the above does for English literature. It covers not only the ordinary literary forms and subjects and the standard writers, but also early travelers' accounts, Colonial newspapers, children's literature, and non-English writings.

The arrangement is: Volume 1, Colonial and Revolutionary Literature; Volume 2, Early National Literature; Volumes 3 and 4, Later National Literature. Very full, important bibliographies, arranged by chapter, are at the ends of Volumes 1, 2, and 4 with the author, title, and subject index.

The 1943 edition of three volumes in one, each with its own annotated table of contents and index, is extremely useful for less scholarly purposes. The extensive bibliographies are omitted from this edition.

Literary History of the United States. 1963. 3rd ed. rev. 2 vols. Vol. 1 is actually two volumes in one. These volumes supplement the *Cambridge History of American Literature* for modern American writings and offer some contemporary opinion of the contents of the *Cambridge History.* Vol. 1 is the literary history, with chapters arranged chronologically, the last chapter being "Since 1945." A table of authors, a bibliography, and an index conclude the volume.

Vol. 2 (actually vol. 3) is a complete bibliography of individual authors' works, being a reprint of the 1959 edition with a supplementary bibliography to bring it up to publication date. Index in each section.

The Reader's Encyclopedia of American Literature. c1962. Covers the United States and Canada for authors, titles, periodicals, literary groups, historical personages, etc. No extensive articles, but sufficient for much information. Criticism appears only in the longer articles. Alphabetical, illustrations, cross references.

Masterplots: Annual Review. 1954–date. Essay-reviews of 100 outstanding books published in the United States during the year. Signed reviews. Alphabetical by title, with an author index.

Oxford Companion to American Literature. 1965. 4th ed. A companion to *reading,* not literature alone. Has much the same scope for American literature as the *Oxford Companion to English Literature* has for English literature, but it is fuller, with much biography. Includes a chronological index in parallel columns, giving literary and social history for America

from 1577 to 1965. Alphabetical by author, title, and subject.
Another in this field is *American Authors and Books, 1640 to the Present Day*, c1962, with very brief information.

POETRY

Encyclopedia of Poetry and Poetics. 1965. International in scope, with history, theory, techniques and criticisms of poetry from earliest times to the present. Articles signed with initials, list of contributors in the front. Alphabetically arranged, with bibliographies at the ends of articles, generous cross references. A monumental and authoritative work.

Oxford Book of American Verse. 1950. A selective anthology of poetry, with an author index and a first line index.

Stevenson's *Home Book of Verse*. 1953. A reprint in two volumes of an earlier edition, paged continuously. A useful collection of American and English poetry, arranged by large subject. Volume 2 has three indexes in the back: (1) authors, (2) first lines, (3) titles. The same compiler's *Home Book of Modern Verse*, 1953, covers the first half of the twentieth century.

QUOTATIONS

Bartlett's *Familiar Quotations*. 1955. Contains quotations from ancient and modern literature. Arranged chronologically by *author* and has two detailed and accurate indexes: (1) Authors alphabetically arranged in the front; (2) Key-word or phrase index in the back. Earlier editions are useful for omissions from this one. Hoyt's *New Cyclopedia of Practical Quotations*, 1947, and Stevenson's *Home Book of Quotations*, 1964, 9th ed., both arranged alphabetically by *subject*, with indexes of authors and of key-words, are two other well-known collections.

Two other helpful ones are the *Oxford Dictionary of Quotations*, 1953, and *FPA Book of Quotations*, c1952. The latter is alphabetical by subject, with an author index. *The Modern Dictionary of Quotations*, c1962, is an English publication and is alphabetical by author with a key-word index.

Some other useful reference books in the field of literature are:

*The Best American Short Stories . . . and the Yearbook of the
American Short Story,* 1915–date.
The Best Plays of . . . The Burns Mantle Yearbook,
1894/99–date.
Masterplots Cyclopedia of Literary Characters, 1963.
*The Reader's Handbook of Famous Names in Fiction,
Allusions, References, Proverbs, Plots, Stories and Poems,*
1957, new rev. ed.
*Cavalcade of the American Novel; From the Birth of the
Nation to the Middle of the Twentieth Century,* c1952.
*Funk and Wagnalls Standard Handbook of Synonyms,
Antonyms and Prepositions,* 1947.
The Synonym Finder, 1961.
Thrall and Hibbard's *Handbook to Literature,* c1960.
Roget's International Thesaurus, c1962.
A Reader's Guide to Literary Terms . . . , c1960.
Brewer's Dictionary of Phrase and Fable, 1963, rev. ed.
Harper's Dictionary of Classical Literature and Antiquities,
c1923.
Oxford Companion to French Literature, 1959.
*The Concise Encyclopedia of English and American Poets and
Poetry,* 1963.

Fine Arts

ART

Encyclopedia of World Art. c1959- . 15 vols. To be completed
in 1968, with 13 vols. having been published through 1966.
Issued simultaneously in English and in Italian through international cooperation between an Italian Editorial Board and
an American Editorial Advisory Committee. Its scope is architecture, sculpture, and painting, encompassing present knowledge of the arts. Authoritative, reliable, prepared by an
international group of specialists in each area of the arts.

Alphabetical, signed articles, long bibliographies, splendid
illustrations. Half of each volume is devoted to full-page
plates, many in color. Vol. 15 will be a full and thoroughly
analytical index.

*History of Art; A Survey of the Major Visual Arts from the
Dawn of History to the Present Day.* c1962. Involved with

events that make the history of art and the scholarly discipline that deals with these events. Good introduction. Arranged in sections: The Ancient World, The Middle Ages, The Renaissance, and The Modern World. Splendid illustrations in black and white and in color, fine classified bibliography in the back, and a full general index.

Larousse Encyclopedia of Modern Art from 1800 to the Present Day: Art and Mankind. c1965. This is really a *survey* covering 150 years and divided into major chronological periods: Classicism and the Romantic Movement, Later Eastern Art, Realism and Impressionism, and Art in the Twentieth Century, with the final chapter on modern-day trends.

Authoritative and well organized, fine illustrations in black and white and in color, exhaustive index but no bibliography. This is the last volume in a series of four, the others being *Larousse Encyclopedia of Prehistoric and Ancient Art, Larousse Encyclopedia of Renaissance and Baroque Art, Larousse Encyclopedia of Byzantine and Medieval Art.*

Encyclopedia of the Arts, c1946, is a useful 10-volume work, no illustrations.

Art through the Ages. c1959. 4th ed. Presents Ancient, European, and Modern Art grouped by periods and countries in clear, chronological accounts of art throughout the world. Extensive bibliographies at the ends of chapters, numerous illustrations primarily black and white. A glossary and a full index are in the back.

Encyclopedia of Painting: Painters and Painting of the World from Prehistoric Times to the Present Day. 1955. Comprehensive presentation of the outstanding painters, movements, techniques, and styles, with a balance between the past and the present. Richly illustrated in black and white and in color, alphabetical, no index, but it has cross references.

Dictionary of Modern Painting. 1964. A panorama of world painting from the impressionists to our times, 1850-1950, translated from the French, in essay form. Alphabetical by painters' names, schools, and art movements; illustrated with color reproductions.

Dictionary of Abstract Painting. 1964. 3rd ed. Another translation from the French, this dictionary is in two parts: Pt. 1—

Illustrated history of abstract painting; pt. 2—Alphabetical arrangement of biographical material on abstract artists, illustrated mostly with reproduction of the artists' works. Bibliography in the back.

Bryan's Dictionary of Painters and Engravers, 1964, 5 vols. and *A Dictionary of Art Terms . . .* , c1962, are two useful reference books.

ARCHITECTURE

A History of Architecture on the Comparative Method. 1961. Arranged in two parts: Pt. 1—Ancient Architecture and the Western Succession; pt. 2—Architecture in the East. Illustrated with many line drawings and photographs, bibliographies at section ends, detailed and extensive index in the back, as well as a list of general reference books on architecture, and a glossary.

Everyman's Concise Encyclopaedia of Architecture. c1959. Limited to *architecture,* does not cover building science, technology, and practice. Very compact and illustrated with line drawings and a few photographs. Alphabetical by name and subject.

Encyclopedia of Modern Architecture. c1963. International in scope, with long, illustrated introductions. Signed articles, many illustrations, bibliographies. In the back are a selective bibliography and an index of architects' names.

Dictionary of Architecture and Building Trades in Four Languages . . . , c1963, is useful also.

DANCE

The Dance Encyclopedia. c1949. Comparatively old but very useful. Long articles signed at the beginning of each, bibliography in the back. Alphabetical, cross references, but no index.

Dictionary of the Dance. c1964. Covers over 100 countries in periods ranging from Ancient Assyria to the present, dealing chiefly with the meanings and aims of the Dance. Alphabetical, illustrated, cross references. Geographical index of subjects relating to the Dance.

Three reference books on Ballet are: *A Dictionary of Ballet,* 1961; *Dictionary of Modern Ballet,* 1959; and *A Dictionary of Ballet Terms,* 1964, 2nd ed.

DRAMA AND THEATRE

Oxford Companion to the Theatre. 1957. 2nd ed. International scope, dealing with theatre in all ages. Representative selection with emphasis on popular theatre rather than literary; meant for those who would prefer seeing a play to reading one, whose interest is as much in production and setting as in literary content. Detailed treatment given to the theatre in the United States.

Alphabetical by subject, with much biography and plentiful cross references. No index. Full bibliography and a supplement in the back.

Digests of Great American Plays. c1961. Digests of complete summaries of more than 100 plays from 1766–1959. Analyzes the theme, plot, characters, social and cultural characteristics of the period, etc. Chronologically arranged.

In the back are a number of appendixes: (1) Alphabetical list of plays, (2) Authors, lyricists, composers, (3) Songs from plays, (4) Distinguished actors and outstanding roles in the plays, (5) Literary origins of the plays, (6) Types of drama represented, etc.

The New Theatre Handbook and Digest of Plays. 1959. For the serious student of the theatre, nice balance between *theatre* and *drama.* Alphabetical arrangement—people, plays, subjects, except articles under Drama and Theatre which are chronologically arranged. The biographies are mostly of current theatre artists.

Theatre Language; A Dictionary of Terms in English of the Drama and Stage from Medieval to Modern Times. c1961. Definitions of words and phrases which constitute the vocabulary of the "legitimate" drama and stage in the United States. Alphabetical, very brief definitions, cross references.

MUSIC AND OPERA

The New Oxford History of Music. 1954–1960. 3 vols. Vol. 1—Ancient and Oriental Music; vol. 2—Early Medieval Music up to 1300; vol. 3—Ars Nova and the Renaissance, 1300–1540. Arranged by chapter, each signed by the author and well documented. Annotated table of contents. Bibliography and index in each volume.

The International Cyclopedia of Music and Musicians. 1964. 9th ed. Outstanding single volume work in this field, international in scope, with emphasis on American music and musicians. Long sections signed by author at beginning of article. At the end of each article on a composer is a full catalog of his works. Alphabetical with cross references. A pronunciation guide is in the back.

The Concise Encyclopaedia of Music and Musicians. c1958. Well illustrated with black and white and color plates. Alphabetical, no index, but many cross references. No bibliographies.

Grove's Dictionary of Music and Musicians. 1954. 5th ed. 9 vols. This has always been a basic reference source in this field. Universal in scope. Alphabetical, cross refrences. Appendixes in vol. 9.

A supplement to the 5th ed. brings the above more nearly up to date, 1961. The 6th ed. will appear eventually.

Encyclopedia of the Great Composers and Their Music. 1962. New rev. ed. 2 vols. Composers of the past and their music. Many useful sections and an index to both volumes. Alphabetical by composers' names.

The Concise Oxford Dictionary of Music. 1964. Biographies of composers and performers of all countries and periods, theoretical terms, terms of expression, general articles on historical phases of music, etc. Alphabetical; no index but many cross references and some illustrations.

Oxford Companion to Music, 1955, is another helpful book, with a very full index and cross references. Two others are *The Harvard Brief Dictionary of Music,* 1960, and *Everyman's Dictionary of Music,* 1958.

Encyclopedia of the Opera. c1963. New enlarged ed. Comprehensive source book about opera and opera performances. Stories of the operas, excerpts from them, biographies, history, characters in opera, etc. Alphabetical.

The World of Music; An Illustrated Encyclopedia, 1963, is a serviceable four-volume work.

The New Milton Cross' Complete Stories of the Great Operas. c1955. Rev. and enlarged ed. Alphabetical by title, with an index. Useful sections in the back. Another is *Opera Guide,* 1965. It is not alphabetical but has an index of names and works and an index of musical terms.

Other useful books in the fields of music and opera are:

The Complete Book of Classical Music, 1961.
Encyclopedia of Concert Music, c1959.
Encyclopedia of Theatre Music . . . , c1961.
The Complete Book of 20th-Century Music, c1959.
The New Edition of the Encyclopedia of Jazz, 1962.
An Introduction to the Language of Music, c1962.
Concise Oxford Dictionary of Opera, 1964.
Crowell's Handbook of the Opera, c1961.
The Opera Companion; A Guide for the Casual Operagoer,
    1961.
The Victor Book of the Operas, 1953.

Religion

Reference books in the field of religion are so numerous that selection for inclusion here is difficult. Only a few are given with annotations; a supplementary list is at the end of this chapter.

GENERAL

The Eleven Religions and Their Proverbial Lore. c1945. A good comparative study with two indexes: (1) subject-matter index; (2) alternative chief-word index.

The World's Great Religions. c1958. Since few people know anything about religions other than their own, this "Special Edition for Young Readers" is useful to adults. Covers Christianity, Judaism, Hinduism, Buddhism, Chinese Philosophy, and Islam. Clearly and understandably presented, exceptionally illustrated in color. Not alphabetical, but has an index.

Religion in the Twentieth Century. 1952. A comparative study of religious faiths existing today, in a series of chapters by different authorities. Very readable and adequately indexed, it is arranged chronologically as far as possible, including a biography of each author and a bibliography for each chapter.

Golden Bough. 1925–1926. Fifteen volumes of information on primitive religions, with a very detailed index. It is supplemented by *Aftermath,* which includes new material published since the third edition of the *Golden Bough* as well as some earlier sources not included in it. Abridged in a one-volume edition, 1956.

ENCYCLOPEDIAS

Encyclopedia of Religion and Ethics. 1908–1927. 12 vols. Contains articles on all religions, ethical systems and movements, religious beliefs and customs, philosophical ideas, moral practices, etc. It is the most comprehensive work in this field. Has an index, signed articles, and full bibliographies. A new edition is in preparation.

New Schaff-Herzog Encyclopedia of Religious Knowledge. 1949–1950. 12 vols. This is one of the most important reference works on the subject in English, Protestant in tone but unbiased. Has an index and excellent bibliographies. Supplemented by *Twentieth Century Encyclopedia of Religious Knowledge,* 1955, in 2 vols.

An Encyclopedia of Religion. c1945. A one-volume work on the theologies of the major religions, denominations, and cults. The broad interpretations of religion, including its role in labor movements, Negro education, penology, etc. are treated, as well as Biblical literature, Christian theology, ecclesiastical history, and many other subjects. Alphabetical, with cross references and bibliographies for long articles, all of which are signed with initials.

Encyclopedia of Bible Life. c1944. A record of the social and economic conditions of the early Christian era, including its agriculture, arts and crafts, professions and trades, homes, nutrition, water supply, etc. Alphabetically arranged by large subject, it has a general index and an index of Biblical quotations. The illustrations and maps are excellent.

Encyclopedia of the Bible. c1965. Translated from the Dutch and originally entitled *Elsevier's Encyclopedie Van de Bijbel.* Alphabetical one-volume work with comparatively brief information, but authoritative. Cross references, no index.

Pictorial Biblical Encyclopedia. 1964. A readable, concise, and authoritative account of the results of Biblical research since World War I, including material from the Dead Sea Scrolls. Voluminous illustrations. Index in the back.

Catholic Encyclopedia. 1907–1912. 15 vols. and an index volume; vol. 17 (1922) and vol. 18 (1950) have been published as supplements. It is the standard work in English for Catholic history, doctrine, and biography. It is very good for questions on medieval literature, history, philosophy, art, etc. This is an authoritative work with long, signed articles, good bibliographies, and illustrations.

The New Catholic Encyclopedia. 1967. 15 vols. Embraces all important knowledge and information having some bearing on or relation to Catholicism and is of great service to the church, the teacher, the student, and the general public. A monumental and authoritative work. Cross references, bibliographies, signed articles, and an index volume .

Universal Jewish Encyclopedia. 1939–1944. An authoritative and popular presentation of Jews and Judaism since the earliest times. Many biographies, including those of living persons, are offered. It is less scholarly than the *Jewish Encyclopedia,* 1901-1906, but accurate and more nearly up to date. Many articles are signed; has some bibliographies. A reading guide and an index are included.

The New Jewish Encyclopedia. c1962. Facts of Jewish religion, history, ethics, literature, and national life. Abundantly illustrated, cross references, no index.

QUOTATIONS

Stevenson's *Home Book of Bible Quotations.* 1949. Done with Stevenson's usual excellence. Arranged by subject and thoroughly indexed, not only for page but for location on the page. Quotations and summaries of famous Bible stories are included. Another one is *A Treasury of Biblical Quotations,* c1948.

ATLAS

Westminster Historical Atlas to the Bible. 1956. Not only an atlas, but a geographical study of the Holy Land in Bible times. Authoritative, with up-to-date maps and articles and two indexes, one to the text and one to the maps. Another, more recent and very good, is the *Rand McNally Bible Atlas,* c1956. Also, *Historical Atlas of the Holy Land,* 1960.

OTHER RELIGIOUS REFERENCE BOOKS

Some other important and useful reference books in religion are:

CONCORDANCES

*Cruden's Complete Concordance to the Old and New
    Testaments . . . with a Concordance to the Apocrypha*, 1930.
Strong's Exhaustive Concordance of the Bible, 1890.
*Thompson and Stock's Complete Concordance to the Bible
    (Douay Version)*, 1945.
Harper's Topical Concordance, 1962.
Nelson's Complete Concordance, 1957.

COMMENTARIES

A Catholic Commentary on Holy Scripture, c1953.
The Interpreter's Bible . . . , 1953–1956. 12 vols.
International Critical Commentary, 1896–1937. 40 vols.
Peake's Commentary on the Bible, 1962.

DICTIONARIES

Attwater's *A Catholic Dictionary*, 1958.
*Concise Dictionary of Religion; A Lexicon of Protestant
    Interpretation*, c1951.
Concise Dictionary of Judaism, c1959.
Encyclopedia Dictionary of the Bible, 1962, 2nd rev. ed.
Harper's Bible Dictionary, c1961.
Hasting's *Dictionary of the Bible*, c1963.
The Interpreter's Dictionary of the Bible, 1962, 4 vols.
The Maryknoll Catholic Dictionary, c1956.
The New Bible Dictionary, c1962.
Oxford Dictionary of the Christian Church, 1927.
Westminster Dictionary of the Bible, 1944.
The Zondervan Pictorial Bible Dictionary, 1963.

YEARBOOKS

American Jewish Yearbook, 1899–date.
The Episcopal Church Annual, 1830–date.
The National Catholic Almanac, 1904–date.
Yearbook of American Churches, 1916–date.

OTHER

Masterpieces of Catholic Literature in Summary Form, c1965,
    2 vols.
*The English Bible in America; A Bibliography of Editions of
    the Bible and the New Testament Published in America
    1777–1957*, 1961.

A Companion to the Bible, 1958.
The Handbook of Biblical Personalities, 1962.
Who's Who in the Bible, c1960.

MAKING
A
BIBLIOGRAPHY

A bibliography is a list of sources of information—books, magazine articles, film strips, theses and dissertations, reference book articles, and so forth.

Many professors require you to submit with your term papers a list of the books or other sources from which you got material. Other professors check your bibliography before you write the paper to make sure that proper sources have been consulted and the best material used. In any case, you cannot escape experience with bibliographies in college, and your initiation will probably come with an English theme. This will put you in good form for the future; you will know what a bibliography is, at least, and run no chance of confusing it with a *biography*.

An *author bibliography* is a list of an author's works. A *subject bibliography* is a list of references on a subject. Either may be *complete* or *selective*. If complete, it includes all references by an author or on a subject; if selective, it includes only some of the possible references, depending upon the purpose for which it is compiled. For instance, a bibliography on *beauty culture* for a chemist differs entirely from one for a debutante, each being selective. Bibliographies with descriptive notes about each reference are called *annotated* bibliographies. The bibliography for a term paper includes all of the sources from which material was gathered.

To help you choose a subject for a paper or for a bibliography, read an article on the subject in an encyclopedia or other reference book. After this survey gives you the scope of the subject, you will have a better idea of where to search for information. Frequently the bibliographies at the end of such articles suggest excellent sources of material. Taking down full bibliographical information when searching for material saves time in the long run, especially when you have decided what you will use. It prevents having to look up material all over again just to get the paging, the exact title of the book, or the author's full name. It is annoying to be far from the library with everything completely prepared except for a few of these essentials, which you failed to copy through negligence or haste.

There are a number of "correct" bibliographical forms, one of which is given below, adequate for all undergraduate purposes, and acceptable for much graduate work, since it is the form used by many graduate schools. An alternate form is given for references from periodicals, which can be used if a simple form is not desired.

You should include the following items, in the order stated:

I. FOR BOOKS:

(1) The name of the author, last name first, (2) the title of the book as it appears on the title page, (3) the edition, if other than the first, (4) the number of volumes in the set if the whole set is used; if a single book, volume is not given, (5) the place of publication, (6) the name of the publisher, (7) the date of publication, and (8) the total paging of the book *if required by your instructor.*

If the author has one given name, write it in full; if more than one, write his first name and then his initial or initials. This applies to all bibliographical references, whether for books, magazine articles, reference book articles, or whatever. (It is also correct to write all of his names in full, but be consistent).

If a book has two or three authors, invert only the first author's name, for alphabetical purposes in the bibliography.

The Bases of Speech

REVISED EDITION

By

GILES WILKESON GRAY, Ph.D.

Director of Speech Laboratory
Louisiana State University

and

CLAUDE MERTON WISE, Ph.D.

Chairman, Department of Speech
Louisiana State University

New York and London

HARPER & BROTHERS PUBLISHERS

Gray, Giles W., and Claude M. Wise. The Bases of Speech.
Rev. ed. New York: Harper, c1946

The

Bases of Speech

Third Edition

by
Giles Wilkeson Gray
and
Claude Merton Wise

Harper & Brothers, Publishers
New York

Gray, Giles W., and Claude M. Wise. The Bases of Speech.
3rd ed. New York: Harper, c1959

Place the first line of each entry in "hanging indention": begin it about four spaces to the left of the following lines in that entry. Capitalize the title of the book (with the exception of the articles *a, the, an,* prepositions and conjunctions unless one appears as the first word in the title), and underline each word separately. If no date of publication or of copyright is given in the book, indicate that fact by *n.d. (No place of publication* and *no publisher* are indicated by *n.p.)* If more than one place of publication is listed, give only the first; the name of the city is sufficient except in cases of possible confusion.

Punctuation: Place a period between the author's name and the title of the book; and another period after the title unless the book is edited, translated, illustrated, or the like—in that case, a comma. A colon goes after the place of publication; a comma, between the publisher and the date. A period is placed after the date and at the end of the reference if other items are given.

Arrangement: Books are usually arranged alphabetically according to the last name of the author. If the author's name is not known, place the book alphabetically by the title. Books *edited* by two or three persons may be alphabetized by the name of the editor or by the title; those edited by more than three persons must be alphabetized by the title.

Abbreviations:

comp.	—compiler, compiled	p.	—page
c	—copyright	pp.	—pages
ed.	—edition, editor, edited	pref.	—preface
enl.	—enlarged	pseud.	—pseudonym
il.	—illustrated, illustrator	rev.	—revised
introd.	—introduction	tr.	—translated, translator
n.d.	—no date	vol.	—volume
n.p.	—no place of publication	vols.	—volumes

EXAMPLES:

A. BOOKS BY ONE AUTHOR:

Spratling, William. A Small Mexican World, il. by the author, foreword by Diego Rivera, introd. by Lesley B. Simpson. Boston: Little, Brown, c1964.

B. BOOKS BY TWO OR THREE AUTHORS:

Gray, Giles W., and Claude M. Wise. The Bases of Speech. 3rd ed. New York: Harper, c1959.

C. AN EDITED TEXT:

1. *An author's works edited by someone else:*

Lincoln, Abraham. Selected Writings and Speeches of Abraham Lincoln, ed. by T. H. Williams. Chicago: Packard [1943]

2. *A collection of different authors' works, edited by one person:*

O'Brien, Edward J. H., ed. 50 Best American Short Stories, 1915–1939. New York: Literary Guild of America, c1939.

3. *Books edited by two or three persons, listed by editors or by title:*

Curie, Eve, Philippe Barres, and Raoul De Roussy de Sales, eds. They Speak for a Nation; Letters from France, tr. by Drake and Denise De Kay. Garden City, N. Y.: Doubleday, Doran, c1941.

They Speak for a Nation; Letters from France, ed. by Eve Curie, Philippe Barres, and Raoul De Roussy de Sales, tr. by Drake and Denise De Kay. Garden City, N. Y.: Doubleday, Doran, c1941.

4. *Books edited by more than three persons:*

Television Advertising and Production Handbook, ed. by Irving Settel, Norman Glenn, and others. New York: Crowell [1953]

D. A TRANSLATION OR AN ILLUSTRATED EDITION:

Schlick, Moritz. Philosophy of Nature, tr. by Amethe von Zeppelin. New York: Philosophical Library, c1949.

II. CORPORATE ENTRIES (see p. 26):

(1) The name of the author of the publication—a person, department, bureau, or organization, (2) the name of the document or publication, (3) the edition, if other than the first, (4) the place of publication, (5) the publisher—not abbreviated, and (6) the date of publication.

If the author or editor of a government publication is a

person, the name of the department or bureau and the number of the bulletin come after the date of publication, in parentheses.

EXAMPLES:

> Densmore, Frances. Pawnee Music. Washington: Government Printing Office, 1929. (U.S. Bureau of American Ethnology. Bulletin 93)
>
> Red Cross. U.S. American National Red Cross. American Red Cross Home Nursing Textbook. 7th ed. New York: Doubleday [c1963]

III. FOR ARTICLES FROM ENCYCLOPEDIAS AND OTHER GENERAL REFERENCE BOOKS:

(1) The name of the author of the article, if known, (2) the name of the article as it appears in the book, (3) the name of the book in which the article appears, (4) the edition, if other than the first, or the date of publication, or the copyright date, (5) the volume number, if one of a set of books, and (6) the inclusive paging of the article.

The first line of each entry is placed in "hanging" indention. The name of the article is enclosed in quotation marks, the name of the book is underlined, each word separately. Words in both titles are capitalized, except articles, prepositions and conjunctions within the title. A period goes after the author's name; a comma, between each of the other items of the entry.

EXAMPLES:

A. ENCYCLOPEDIAS:

> "Etiquette," Compton's Pictured Encyclopedia, c1960, vol. 4, pp. 492–499.
>
> Mabbott, John D. "Ethics, History of—Modern Ethics," Encyclopaedia Britannica, c1959, vol. 8, pp. 769–778.

B. YEARBOOKS:

> Ley, Willy. "Space Flight—Astronautics—The Principles of Space Flight," Americana Annual, c1959, pp. 691–698.

C. BIOGRAPHICAL DICTIONARIES:

> Kirk, Richard R. "King, Grace Elizabeth," Dictionary of American Biography, 1933, vol. 10, pp. 389–390.
>
> "Von Braun, Wernher," Who's Who in America, 1958–1959, c1958, p. 2856.

D. BOOKS OF QUOTATIONS:

Instead of the name of the article, give the first line of the quotation, followed by three dots (. . .) to denote incompleteness:

> Irving, Washington. "Your true dull minds are generally preferred for public employ . . . ," Bartlett's Familiar Quotations, 11th ed., p. 343.

E. THESIS OR DISSERTATION:

> Foote, John T. "The History of Education in Louisiana." (Unpublished M.A. thesis, Louisiana State University, 1933.)

Substitute M.S. for Master of Science thesis; Ph.D. for doctoral dissertation; or use appropriate abbreviation of degree, if other than these given.

IV. FOR ARTICLES FROM PERIODICALS:

A. MAGAZINE ARTICLES:

(1) The name of the author of the article, if known, (2) the name of the article, (3) the name of the magazine in which the article appears, (4) the volume of the magazine, (5) the date, and (6) the inclusive paging of the article.

The first line of each entry is placed in "hanging indention." The volume number of the magazine is given in Arabic numerals; complete numerals are given for the inclusive paging.

Punctuation: Put a period after the author's name. The name of the article is capitalized (except *a, the, an,* prepositions and conjunctions) and enclosed in quotation marks. A comma goes between the name of the article and the name of the magazine. Capitalize the name of the magazine and underline each word separately. A comma goes between the name of the magazine and the volume (abbreviated) number, but no comma between volume and date, which is enclosed in parentheses. If it is a monthly magazine, no comma between month and year. Comma between date and paging; period at end of reference.

Some magazines are published quarterly; if so, put *Spring, Summer, Fall,* or *Winter* in the place of the month in the date.

Arrangement: Articles and stories from magazines and collections are arranged alphabetically according to the author's last name, if known; otherwise, they are by titles.

Examples:

> Brownlow, Cecil. "The War in Vietnam—Special Report: VNAF Seeks Means to Train Own Pilots," Aviation Week & Space Technology, vol. 82 (June 7, 1965), pp. 62–63.
> "Minding Our Manners," Newsweek, vol. 52 (Aug. 11, 1958), pp. 90–91.
> Polo, Charles. Review of The Status Seekers, by Vance Packard, Atlantic Monthly, vol. 203 (May 1959), p. 91.
> Hicks, Granville. "Voyage of Life," review of Ship of Fools, by Katherine Anne Porter, Saturday Review, vol. 54 (March 31, 1962), pp. 15–16.

ALTERNATE FORM FOR PERIODICAL REFERENCES

The differences between the above and the following forms are in the volume and date indications. Many scholarly researchers use the following form, even though many students and even library workers have difficulty in reading Roman numerals and in transposing them to and from the Arabic ones. In this form only the *year* is given for journals and other periodicals which are published quarterly. Use capital Roman numerals for volume. Do not use *p.* or *pp.* for paging.

Examples:

> Brownlow, Cecil. "The War in Vietnam—Special Report: VNAF Seeks Means to Train Own Pilots," Aviation Week & Space Technology, LXXXII (June 7, 1965), 62–63.
> "Minding Our Manners," Newsweek, LII (Aug. 11, 1958), 90–91.

B. *NEWSPAPER ARTICLES:*

Newspaper-article references have the same form as magazine-article references, except that a newspaper reference cites the *page* and *column*, and occasionally the *section*. There is no volume.

EXAMPLES:

> Atkinson, Brooks. "Plays and People—From Off-Broadway to Moses' Central Park," The New York Times (July 14, 1959), sec. 2, p. 1, col. 1.
>
> "60,000 Members of Long Island Women's Clubs Federation Favor New York Theatres League Plan for Early Evening Curtain Once a Week," The New York Times (June 2, 1959), p. 40, col. 1.

SAMPLE BIBLIOGRAPHY:

Space Flight

A Bibliography

Books

Branley, Franklyn M. Exploration of the Moon. Garden City, N. Y.: National History Press, 1964.

Corliss, William R. Space Probes and Planetary Exploration. Princeton, N. J.: Van Nostrand [c1965]

Deutsch, Ralph. Orbital Dynamics of Space Vehicles. Englewood Cliffs, N. J.: Prentice-Hall [c1963]

Gallant, Roy A. Man's Reach into Space, il. by Lee J. Ames. Rev. ed. Garden City, N. Y.: Doubleday [1964]

Leondes, Cornelius T., and Robert W. Vance. Lunar Missions and Exploration. New York: Wiley [c1964]

"Space Development," World Almanac, 1966, pp. 44–45.

Stehling, Kurt R. "Space Exploration," Americana Annual, 1966, pp. 615–629.

Von Braun, Wernher. "Space Vehicles," Encyclopedia Americana, c1964, vol. 25, pp. 320o–321b.

Periodicals

David, Heather M. "Longer Manned Flights Now Seen Safe," Missiles and Rockets, vol. 18 (March 21, 1966), p. 31.

"Gemini 9: Launching Preparations Proceed Smoothly," The New York Times, (May 16, 1966), p. 10, col. 1.

"Meanwhile, NASA Builds a Moonport," Fortune, vol. 73 (Feb. 1966), pp. 144–149.

Murray, Bruce C., and Merton E. Davies. "Comparison of U. S. and Soviet Efforts to Explore Mars," Science, vol. 151 (Feb. 25, 1966), pp. 945–954.

Von Braun, Wernher. "Bonanzas on the Way to the Moon," Popular Science Monthly, vol. 188 (March 1966), pp. 106–107.

INDEX

INDEX

Guide to the Best Fiction, 47
Guide to the Best Historical Fiction, 47
Guide to the Best Historical Novels and Tales, 47
Guide to the Literature of Mathematics and Physics . . ., 44
Guide to the Musical Arts . . ., 46
Guide to the Performing Arts, 47
Guide to the Use of United Nations Documents, A, 53
Guides to Information Sources in Science and Technology, 45

H

Hackh's Chemical Dictionary, 75
Hammond's Ambassador World Atlas, 83
Handbook of Biblical Personalities, The, 105
Handbook of Chemistry and Physics, 69
Handbook of Geophysics, 69-70
Handbook of Geophysics for Air Force Designers, 70
Handbook of Latin American Studies, 39, 42
Handbook to Literature, 96
Handbooks, 63-71, 72, 104
Harper Encyclopedia of Science, The, 73
Harper's Bible Dictionary, 104
Harper's Dictionary of Classical Literature and Antiquities, 96
Harper's Topical Concordance, 104
Harvard Brief Dictionary of Music, The, 100
Hasting's Dictionary of the Bible, 104
Historical Abstracts, 54
Historical Atlas of the Holy Land, 103
Historical Atlas of the United States, 83
Historical fiction, 47
Historical Fiction Guide . . ., 47
Historical Statistics of the United States, 1610-1957, 68
History, 78-80
History of Architecture on the Comparative Method, A, 98
History of Art . . ., 96-97
History of Latin America from the Beginning to the Present, 80
History of Technology, 72-73
Home Book of Bible Quotations, 103

Home Book of Modern Verse, 75
Home Book of Quotations, 95
Home Book of Verse, 95
How To Locate Educational Information and Data, 46
Hoyt's New Cyclopedia of Practical Quotations, 95
Hyphenated words, in card catalog, 22

I

Identical names, filed in card catalog,
Illustration Index, 46
Illustrations:
  list of, in books, 10
  listed in bibliographical references, 108
  on catalog card, 23
Illustrator:
  in bibliographical references, 110
  on catalog card, 23
  on title page, 9
Imprint, 23
Index:
  abbreviations in, 39-51
  arrangement of, 37-38
  cross references, 39, 41
  in books, 11
  kinds, in books, 11-12
  to encyclopedias, 11-12, 59
  to magazines, 12, 37-52
  to maps, 82-84
  to newspapers, 52-53
  to periodicals, 12, 37-52
  to plays, short stories, poems, 47-49
  to poetry collections, 49, 95
  volume, 12, 59, 61
Index Medicus, 45
Index to Book Reviews in the Humanities, An, 51-52
Index to Full Length Plays, 48
Index to Jewish Periodicals, 50
Index to Latin American Periodical Literature, 42
Index to Latin American Periodicals; Humanities and Social Sciences, 43
Index to One-Act Plays, 48
Index to Plays, 48
Index to Plays in Collections, 49
Index to Poetry, 49
Index to Poetry and Recitations, 49
Index to Religious Periodical Literature, 50

WORK
SHEETS

THE CARD CATALOG

SUBJECT OF BIBLIOGRAPHY: **LAST NAME**   **FIRST NAME**

....

INSTRUCTOR ....   DAY AND HOUR ....

PERIODICAL INDEXES

SUBJECT OF BIBLIOGRAPHY: LAST NAME   FIRST NAME

....

INSTRUCTOR ....   DAY AND HOUR ....

ENCYCLOPEDIAS

YEARBOOKS AND HANDBOOKS

SCIENCE AND TECHNOLOGY

HISTORY AND THE SOCIAL SCIENCES

BIOGRAPHICAL DICTIONARIES

HUMANITIES

Literature, Fine Arts, Religion